Inspiration

to

LIVE YOUR™ MAGIC!

75 Inspiring Biographies

LARRY ANDERSON

Book Title: Inspiration to Live Your MAGIC!
Book Subtitle: 75 Inspiring Biographies
Author: Larry Anderson

Copyright © 2011 LIAP Media Corp.
Live Your MAGIC!™ trade mark pending

Publisher

LIAP Media Corp.
1112-95 Street S.W.
Edmonton, Alberta, Canada
T6X 0A7

Visit our website at www.LiveYourMagic.com

Book Cover Design: Allen Mohr
Portrait Illustrations: Sayan Chakraborty
Book Page Layout Design: Jana Rade

ISBN-978-0-9869417-0-2

Printed in the United States of America

This book is dedicated to my daughter Jennifer, my son Stephen, and the youth of the world. Live your MAGIC!

Larry Anderson's own story is compelling and inspiring enough, never mind the stories contained in Inspiration to Live Your MAGIC!™.

From young people with a belief that child labour is wrong, to world class philosophers, Larry Anderson captures the spirit and essence of inspiration. In this volume you will find stories of children, women and men who followed their dreams. These inspired individuals changed their communities, their nation and the world. From politics, diplomacy, entertainment, the arts and science, their stories demonstrate the triumph of the human spirit.

From the slums of Calcutta, to the halls of Government, the Courts and the glitz of Las Vegas, these individual stories are victories of faith over fear.

A must read for all, this book is truly inspiring.

—Robert Philp , Provincial Court Judge , Edmonton, Alberta, Canada

This book is filled with real life stories of courage, leadership, wisdom and love. A must read for all young people. Our world is a better place because of the choices each of these people made in their life journey.

—Jay Ball, President & CEO, Junior Achievement of Northern Alberta

I love the way "Inspiration to Live Your MAGIC!™ is written. It captures your attention and is easy to read and understand. I not only learned but it evoked a yearning inside me to live my own magic. Thank you.

—Jeannie Lungard, Teacher, Psychologist

These seventy-five biographies showcase people from all age groups, backgrounds and cultures. What they share is a passion and commitment to make their dreams come true and to make a difference for others in the process. Read Inspiration to Live Your MAGIC!™, you will be inspired.

—Bill Trainor, Retired Teacher

Acknowledgements

First, I acknowledge the support of my wife Janet, who encouraged me to write a book, and accommodated and protected my need for solitude to read, think, and write. She also acted as a sounding board for all of my ideas, giving her honest opinion. I am grateful.

Next, I thank my business partners, especially Lewis Nakatsui and Mike Gendron, and my staff, especially Percy Pouliot, Ray Mitchell, Wesley Gunderson, and Stephen Anderson, who allowed, supported, and encouraged me to set aside Wednesdays, beginning in January 2000, to explore my passion for writing.

For this book, *Inspiration to Live Your MAGIC!*, I thank Glen Stone for his research into each inspiring life I selected, finding details that would convey the essence of each journey in 400 words. I also thank Cathy Reed and Mary W. Walters for editing and assistance in organizing the biographies. You have significantly improved this book.

Finally, I want to thank three people who believed in and encouraged me as a writer. I met Dave Kirk at five years of age at Daily Vacation Bible Camp in the summer of 1953, and he ended up in my grade one class that fall and in every class until grade nine, when I went to a different school. We were both outsiders and became the closest of friends, and remained so until his premature death in 2005 from cancer. He was the one person I shared my journals with throughout my journey, and he repeatedly told me I needed to write a book.

Two other friends, Gerry Riskin and Mary W. Walters, both published authors and friends from university in the 1970s, have consistently encouraged me to write a book. They provided the confidence when mine waned.

Thank you all.

Foreword

In my work as a teacher of students with learning challenges, I have myself learned much from my charges. For example, I learned that many such students remain trusting and maintain the courage to keep on trying, receptive to a teacher's efforts to help them meet their challenges. Other students, however, become discouraged and lose their trust in both their own competence and that of anyone else to assist them. I realized that if educators did not do something to rebuild students' confidence and give them the means to overcome their difficulties, it mattered little if they learned literacy and numeracy skills while nevertheless remaining disempowered persons adrift without hope.

Larry Anderson went through different kinds of challenges in his early life, and was close to losing hope in himself and in his dreams. But he found the means to become empowered, through reading, through dreaming, through the self-reflection writing journals required. Thus, coming to understand the power of hope and belief in one's ability to take charge of one's life, Larry has committed himself to communicating this message.

Life is and always will be full of challenges, but the belief that they can be overcome with persistence, determination, and courage is essential to one's well-being. Each person does have a contribution to make, and one's mindset determines whether that contribution is positive and effective or negligible and wasted. By reading stories such as those in Inspiration to Live Your MAGIC!™, and recognizing the long and arduous journeys that often must be taken to pursue one's dream, personal reflection can inspire one to strive to reach their potential and live the best life possible.

Judy Craig, Retired Teacher, Principal and Administrator

Preface

I wrote this book to keep a promise I made to a twelve-year-old boy in 1959.

The young boy had only two memories of his biological father. He remembered being beaten with a belt at six years of age because he wouldn't drink his milk. And he remembered his mother sobbing because of the abuse.

One day, when he was seven, his biological father was gone. There was no explanation. The boy didn't care.

A few years later, his mother married another man, who became his stepfather and who later adopted the boy. This man was kind and supportive, but he was an alcoholic. Many nights, their tiny home was filled with screaming and arguing, usually about money and alcohol, which grew louder as the drinking continued.

One such night in the middle of winter, the boy lay trembling in his bed in the open basement. There were no curtains on the small windows and all around him the laundry was hanging on lines to dry. A car passed by and the headlights shone through the windows, creating shadow monsters of the laundry. The boy pulled the blankets over his head and retreated into his dreams. That night, he made a promise to himself: if he ever figured out how to make his dreams come true, he would share what he had learned with others.

That young boy was me. I had three dreams: to find a girlfriend and have a loving family; to start my own business and make money; and to travel the world.

At sixteen, I dropped out of school and left home, to escape the chaos and pursue my dreams.

At nineteen, I was a lonely, penniless, unemployed high school dropout, living in a basement room and clinging to the hope that my dreams could still come true.

In my early twenties, one profound insight changed the course of my life in an instant. I realized my past did not have to define my future. I began *the journey to live* my *MAGIC!*

At sixty-three, I'm living my dreams. My wife Janet and I have been married for thirty-five years. We have two wonderful adult children, Jennifer and Stephen. I started my first business in 1974, which became part of a business group in 1978 of which I'm president and CEO.

Janet and I are financially independent, and we travel six months a year. We have visited every continent except Antarctica (the Antarctic seas are too rough for Janet, but we waved to Antarctica from the Strait of Magellan as we passed the southern tip of South America). This book is part of keeping the promise I made to the twelve-year-old me.

For over forty years, since I was nineteen, I have kept a journal. These journals were sometimes ten-cent coil notebooks, sometimes leather hardcover volumes, but more typically were small, hardcover notebooks I would carry in my pocket.

In order to answer the question, "How did I make my dreams come true?" I have reviewed my journals five times, and the process of distilling the answer has taken ten years.

In the end, the answer has three parts: inspiration, wisdom, and the journey. Together, these three parts show you how to live *your* MAGIC!

I have written three books that together provide the answer:

- *Inspiration to Live Your MAGIC! 75 Inspiring Biographies* (which is this book)
- *Wisdom to Live Your MAGIC! Life Lessons from 50 Amazing Teachers*
- *The Journey to Live Your MAGIC! Five Gifts, Five Choices, Six Tools*

To publish these books and other media resources, I established a publishing company called LIAP Media Corp. LIAP Media Corp. is a social enterprise. I receive no compensation, and one hundred percent of all royalties and profits will be donated to charity.

It is my new dream that these three books and other media resources will help you and others to live your dreams, through embarking on *The Journey to Live* Your *MAGIC!*

Larry Anderson, April 2011

Introduction

The most powerful story we tell is the story we tell to ourselves about our self.

In my youth, my story was based on my experience. In gym class, I was always the last one picked for teams. "Who will take Larry?" the gym teacher would ask. Girls told me, "I just want to be friends," but I wanted to be more than friends. My marks in school were not impressive. I passed, but that was about it.

After I dropped out of school at sixteen, I left home and got a job. Things seemed better at first. My jobs would seem interesting and fun at the beginning, but they soon became drudgery. And the pay didn't support much of a lifestyle. I might have accepted that if I could have seen a future, but I couldn't.

The problem was: I was an expert on who I was not, but I didn't have a clue who I was. My story about me was about who I wasn't and what I couldn't do. The truth was that I felt sorry for myself.

Clearly, the story I was telling myself about me was holding me back. What I needed was some perspective, and I got that perspective from reading the biographies of Anne Frank, Thomas Edison, and Benjamin Franklin.

My troubles were tiny compared to those of thirteen-year-old Anne Frank hiding in an attic from the Nazis. Yet her response was, "I don't think of all the misery, but of the beauty that remains," and, "Where there's hope, there's life."

I began to have hope, too.

Some people said that Thomas Edison had failed more than any man who had ever lived. Yet that wasn't how he saw it. He said, "I haven't failed. I have just found 10,000 ways that won't work. Our greatest weakness lies in giving up. The most certain way to succeed is to try just one more time."

I began to see my mistakes and "failures" as learning experiences.

What amazed me about Benjamin Franklin was that he admitted his faults and then shared his plan for self-improvement. He detailed how he'd use a journal to monitor his progress and keep himself on track.

I began to keep a journal and to think about how I could improve myself. The story I was telling myself about myself started to improve. I decided to complete my high school education.

Every person in this collection inspires, by their response to challenges (and some of them face incredible challenges), by their commitment to serving humanity, and by staying committed to their values.

I believe every person who reads these stories will be inspired.

Table of Contents

List of Biographies According to Various Categories

Note: These inspiring individuals have been grouped into general categories as a way of highlighting their predominant interests and achievements. However, the reader will see that a significant number of them fit in several, or even many, categories.

Artists

A. Y. Jackson	24
Grandma Moses	94
Walt Disney	238

Authors

Anne Frank	48
Beatrix Potter	54
J. K. Rowling	109
Malcolm Gladwell	135
Maya Angelou	153
Paulo Coelho	191
Robert Munsch	200
Stephen Leacock	229

Singers/Songwriters

Celine Dion	66
Diane Warren	75
Gordon Lightfoot	91
Shania Twain	219

Other Music/Media

Andrew Lloyd Webber	45
Gustavo Dudamel	97
Joseph Pulitzer	122
Oprah Winfrey	188

A. Y. Jackson

Once ridiculed by critics, Canadian painter A.Y. Jackson is now considered the pioneer of modern landscape art. He is also the founder of the famous Canadian Group of Seven.

The first time A.Y. Jackson and his artist friends had a show of their paintings, critics called them "the product of a deranged mind." It's a good thing that Jackson believed in himself and his abilities; otherwise, he might not have gone on to be one of the most successful and respected artists in Canadian history.

Alexander Young Jackson (everyone called him A. Y.) was born to a poor family in Montreal in 1882. His father abandoned them when he was young, and A.Y. had to go to work at age twelve to help support his brothers and sisters.

Working in a print shop, he became interested in art, and eventually he saved up enough money to travel and study in Europe.

After returning to Canada, he began to paint landscapes in a fresh new style. Other young artists took notice, and A.Y. Jackson soon had a group of friends who not only loved to paint, but also aspired to change the traditional way in which landscapes were painted.

Jackson had faith in himself and his fellow artists; he felt they could turn the art world on its head. He and several other artists decided to try an unusual experiment. Traveling by train, and living together in a boxcar as it rolled across northern Ontario, they painted everything they saw.

The "Group of Seven," as they called themselves, put the results of the tour together to create an art show in Toronto in 1920. That was the show where the critics called the paintings "art gone mad."

But this did not deter A. Y.; he was convinced that the Group of Seven was on to something great. He kept painting, traveling, and exhibiting, and although it took many years, his modern style started to catch on and his work became increasingly popular.

By the time he died in 1974 at the age of eighty-two, A.Y. Jackson was acknowledged as a painting genius and a pioneer of modern landscape art. He and the other painters of the Group of Seven are among the most famous artists in Canadian history, with an entire museum and art gallery dedicated to their work.

Jackson could have chosen to listen to the critics and given up his bold new ideas, but he remained confident and followed his dream.

Aaron Moser

After a serious accident not
only ended Aaron Moser's
junior hockey career but
made him a quadriplegic, he
created a research foundation
dedicated to finding a cure
for spinal cord injuries.

Some Canadian patriots get themselves a maple leaf tattoo. Aaron Moser got two maple leafs built into his custom-made wheelchair—the one he used to help carry the Olympic torch.

It was an incredibly proud moment when Moser, who calls himself a "super patriot," helped carry the torch around the arena at the opening of the 2010 Winter Olympic Games in Vancouver. It was also a tribute to him and his courage.

Aaron was only seventeen years old when tragedy struck during a 1998 local junior league hockey game in British Columbia. He was checked into the boards, hit head first, and broke his neck. Aaron's spinal cord was cut, leaving him a quadriplegic; he has no feeling or movement below his chest.

For Aaron, who was such an athletic and active guy, it was a brutal blow. For his family, it meant adapting their lives and their home to support him, and help him adjust to his new life. It also meant extra expenses.

Aaron Moser's family, friends, and the entire community pulled together. They set up a trust fund to cover the renovations, equipment, supplies, and other expenses. Soon, the trust fund was swamped with donations—not just from people in the area who knew Aaron, but also from people throughout the world of hockey.

They weren't just motivated by the tragedy; they were inspired by the way the teenager handled the shocking change to his life. Aaron refused to complain about his fate or to give up hope. He kept insisting that he would work hard enough and long enough to walk again.

The trust fund and Moser's courage kept attracting donations. After a while, there was enough money not only to help Aaron Moser, but also to set up a foundation in his name—a non-profit group dedicated to helping find a cure for him and others with spinal cord injuries.

Every year, Moser and dedicated volunteers run a golf tournament and other activities to raise money for spinal cord injury research. As of this writing, they have brought in more than $400,000. And every year, they help researchers get a little closer to a cure.

As Moser always says, "I have no doubt that one day I will walk again!"

Abraham Lincoln

A lawyer and an advocate for making slavery illegal, Abraham Lincoln was president of the U.S. during the American Civil War that ended with the abolishment of slavery.

It's not always easy to do the right thing, especially when some people are threatening to kill you if you don't back down!

But Abraham Lincoln was the kind of person who stuck to his principles, no matter what.

Abe Lincoln was always known for "doing the right thing." His small store in Kentucky became the most popular in town because people knew they could trust him. That's how he earned his nickname—"Honest Abe."

All through his life, Lincoln valued integrity more than anything else. He insisted that people who worked for him must be honest and fair.

Although he was born in poverty, Lincoln pulled himself up through life. He studied at night to become a lawyer. He was popular and well-liked enough to get into politics, and that's where Abe Lincoln's sense of what was right and wrong rose to the top.

Slavery was still legal in the United States, and Lincoln was one of many people who believed it was simply wrong. He gave powerful speeches calling for an end to slavery.

The issue was threatening to tear the country apart by the time Lincoln was elected president. The southern and northern states had opposing views on the subject and the U.S. Civil War began.

It was a long war with many casualties. Soon, Lincoln was unpopular in many parts of the north; in the south, he was simply hated.

Even after the northern forces won the war and Lincoln was president of the whole country again, many people in the south wished him dead. That hatred only got worse when Lincoln kept his word and freed the slaves. But even though he was getting death threats, Honest Abe stuck to his principles.

One night Lincoln went with his wife to watch a play. At the theater, an actor who didn't like Lincoln's politics shot and killed him. It was a great shock to the nation. The country had lost its strong but gentle leader.

That was more than 140 years ago, but Abraham Lincoln is still remembered as one of the greatest leaders in American history—the man who ended slavery in the United States by doing the right thing, no matter what the cost.

Albert Schweitzer

Albert Schweitzer became a doctor so he could devote the rest of his life to helping people who most needed help. He also traveled the world, advocating for peace and "reverence for life," and won the Nobel Peace Prize for his humanitarian work.

"Do something wonderful with your life," said Albert Schweitzer. "People may imitate you!"

Dr. Schweitzer lived out those words, using his life to help untold thousands of people and to set an example that still inspires the world today.

As a child in the late 1800s, Albert Schweitzer showed an incredible talent for music. By the time he was a young man, he was not only giving popular concerts on the pipe organ, he had become an acknowledged world expert on building organs, interpreting classical music, and making musical recordings.

He made a very good living with his music, but Schweitzer was also a deep thinker when it came to religion and living a good, worthwhile life. He wrote influential books about Jesus Christ and Christian philosophy, and he decided that when he turned thirty years old, he would give up his career and devote the rest of his life to helping other people.

As planned, he quit working at age thirty and went back to school. His family and friends thought he was crazy, but Schweitzer had decided to become a doctor. He figured that was the best route to being able to help others in need.

After getting his medical degree, Dr. Schweitzer raised enough money by playing more concerts to set off for the poor African country of Gabon, where there was a critical shortage of medical care. He and his wife traveled more than 300 kilometers up the Ogooué River and set up a makeshift hospital.

People came from hundreds of kilometers around to Dr. Schweitzer's little one-room medical miracle—the only hospital and doctor that most of them had ever seen. He and his wife, Helene, worked themselves to exhaustion. They were forced to stop when World War I broke out when, as Germans working in French territory, they were taken prisoner.

After the war, Dr. Schweitzer went back to Gabon, re-built the abandoned hospital, and resumed his free medical care for anyone who needed it. For another forty years, until his death in 1963, he spent most of his time in Gabon. He spent the rest of his time traveling the world, raising money and encouraging other people to follow his example.

Albert Schweitzer was awarded the Nobel Peace Prize in 1952—not just for his hospital work, but also for his personal philosophy—"Reverence for Life"— that encouraged everyone to respect others and recognize their right to life.

Alfred Nobel

Can you imagine reading your
own obituary in the newspaper?
What would people say about
you? Alfred Nobel got the chance
to read his own death notice,
and he didn't like what he saw.

★ 37 ★

Alfred Nobel was a very wealthy and successful man. He had become an expert in chemistry and invented three of the most commonly used explosives in the world—dynamite, gelignite (used in mining) and ballistite, which is still used as a rocket propellant today.

With the huge fortune he made from these inventions, Nobel bought an engineering company called Bofors and turned it into an arms manufacturer. He made another enormous fortune designing cannons and guns and selling them around the world.

Then, in 1888, Alfred's brother died while visiting France. A French newspaper thought it was Alfred who had died and they published an obituary that began like this:

THE MERCHANT OF DEATH IS DEAD

Dr. Alfred Nobel, who became rich by finding ways to kill more people faster than ever before, died yesterday....

Alfred Nobel was shocked. Was this what people thought of him? Was this the legacy he would leave to the world? That's when he decided to use his vast wealth to make a positive difference.

Nobel set up a foundation with $250 million dollars in funding. Every year the foundation would consult the leading experts in the world and hand out prizes to people who had made great contributions to humanity. There would be prizes for sciences, for literature, and for promoting peace.

Today the Nobel Prizes are probably the best-known and most prestigious awards in the world. They have been awarded to great scientists, authors and activists and helped draw attention to many outstanding works and worthy causes.

Nobel set up his foundation in 1895: just in time to influence his own obituary. He died only a year later.

The Nobel Prizes accomplished his wish; they created a very different legacy for him than a reputation as "The Merchant of Death." He is not remembered as an explosives inventor or arms dealer, but as one of the greatest philanthropists of all time.

He is also a great example of how it is never too late to change your life and help make the world a better place.

Alice Waters

Besides being a world-renowned chef and creator of the famous California restaurant Chez Panisse, Alice Waters runs a national campaign promoting organic food and healthy eating for children.

When famous people from Hollywood travel through Berkeley, California, there is only one place to eat: Chez Panisse. It's been named the best restaurant in the United States, and one of the best in the entire world.

The creator of this remarkable eating-place is Alice Waters, who has been voted one of the top chefs on the planet, and is given credit for popularizing organic food in North America.

Waters actually set out to be a teacher, and was studying education in France when she discovered fine food and the fact that organic food, locally grown without chemicals, makes a huge difference in cooking.

Back home, while working as a teacher, she continued studying, cooking, and making delicious meals for friends . . . and their friends . . . and their friends' friends. It wasn't long before she thought of opening a restaurant to serve her organic food to everyone.

Within a few years, Chez Panisse was a sensation, and Waters' ideas for fresh, healthy food spread to other restaurants, and then to supermarkets and kitchens across North America. She changed the way that many people think about and prepare their food.

Some people might be satisfied with having legions of happy clients, a worldwide reputation, and a series of bestselling books. Other people might have expanded into more restaurants, TV shows, and other ways of building on their wealth and fame—but not Alice Waters. For her, the money and recognition are only tools; it's how you use them that counts.

So, now that she has played a big role in making organic food popular and available, Waters has decided to make another difference in the world. She is using her fame, experience, and knowledge for something else she strongly believes in—helping children.

That's why you'll see one of the world's best chefs going into schools to teach kids (and their parents) about healthy eating and organic food. It's part of her national campaign to fight obesity and other health problems caused by bad eating habits that people develop when they are young. Her dream is to help everyone enjoy a better quality of life through better eating.

So, in the end, Alice Waters is still following her dream of teaching and helping young people.

Amelia Earhart

A record-setting aviation
pioneer and adventurer,
Amelia Earhart was a celebrity
and advocate for women's
equality in the early 1900s.

Millie and Pidge were two unusual little girls. Growing up in the 1860s in Kansas, their mother let them run wild like the neighborhood boys—something that just wasn't done in those days. Millie and her sister became fearless tomboys: climbing trees, collecting bugs, and helping their uncle build a home-made (and very dangerous!) wooden roller coaster.

Full of self-confidence, Amelia (Millie's real name) grew up determined to do something great with her life. She just didn't know what it was going to be.

One answer seemed to come during World War I, when Earhart visited her sister in Toronto and ended up volunteering as a nurse at a military hospital. Right after the war, a worldwide flu pandemic killed millions of people in 1918. Earhart kept nursing but got sick herself, and spent nearly a year recovering in the hospital.

Then, something else happened in Toronto that changed Amelia Earhart's life. She watched one of the first annual air shows at the famous Canadian National Exhibition. The pilot of a biplane swooped down low and flew right over her head. From that moment, she was hooked on airplanes.

Back home in Kansas, Earhart took her first airplane ride and announced that she was going to learn to fly. Working every job she could get, Amelia saved up the money for lessons and became only the sixteenth woman in the world to get her international flying license.

Amelia Earhart became somewhat of a celebrity and set out to promote flying, especially for women. Her fame skyrocketed after she became the first woman to fly across the Atlantic Ocean, even though she was little more than a passenger.

After that, Earhart started setting her own records. She became the first woman to fly across North America and back, set a new world altitude record, and became the first woman to fly solo across the Atlantic.

By this time, she was a major star—writing books, making celebrity appearances, and designing her own line of clothes. She used her fame to promote flying as a form of transportation, and constantly worked for equality for women, not just in the air, but in all aspects of life.

Amelia Earhart was one of the most famous people in the world when she disappeared during her greatest adventure—flying around the world. Her fate is still a mystery.

Andrew Lloyd Webber

Composer, writer, and producer of the most popular musicals of all time, Andrew Lloyd Webber is an Oscar, Grammy, and Tony Award winner, and a huge contributor to the arts in Britain.

Music was in Andrew Lloyd Webber's genes. His father was a classical composer, and his mother played both the violin and piano; Webber's younger brother grew up to be a world-renowned solo cello player.

So it's not surprising that Andrew loved music as a child, and showed a remarkable natural talent. By age nine, he was composing suites of classical music.

Among Andrew's talented family members was his Aunt Viola, an actress who introduced him to the world of theater and took him to see many plays and musical shows. The bright little boy fell in love with the stage and dreamed of being involved in show business.

Andrew was a top student in school and went off to the famed Oxford University to study history. But his love of music and the theater was so strong that he realized he would never be happy unless he followed his passion. He switched to the Royal College of Music, determined to pursue his dream.

There are always many bright young musicians trying to make a living composing music, but Andrew Lloyd Webber stood out from the crowd by using two important aspects of his artistic background—the discipline and power of classical music, and the fun and appeal of the popular theater.

The musicals he created from that artistic fusion include the most popular of all time. His shows, including Cats, Joseph and the Amazing Technicolor Dreamcoat, Evita, The Phantom of the Opera, and Jesus Christ, Superstar, have set box-office records, become popular films, and generated such hit songs as "Memory," "The Music of the Night," and "Don't Cry for Me, Argentina."

With one smash hit after another, Webber was instrumental in bringing musicals back into popularity. He has won a long list of awards, including an Oscar, four Grammies, and seven Tony Awards.

Webber has invested some of the hundreds of millions of dollars he has made (he's among the richest people in Britain) into buying theaters, supporting upcoming playwrights and composers, and creating a charitable foundation.

He has contributed so much to the arts in Britain that the Queen knighted him, and later made him a baron. Sir Andrew Lloyd Webber is still following his passion for musical theater, creating new shows that tour the world and bring his unique brand of music to new generations of fans.

Anne Frank

Author of a diary that chronicled
the fate of a Jewish family in
Nazi Germany, teenager Anne
Frank died in a concentration
camp; but, decades later,
her diary was published in
more than sixty languages.

Being a Jew in Nazi Germany was a horrific fate. Adolf Hitler and the Nazis took away the Jews' jobs, property, and rights, then began sending them to concentration camps where they worked under horrible conditions and were beaten, starved, and often killed en masse in gas ovens.

Anne Frank was just four years old when the Nazis came to power, and her family wisely fled from Germany to Holland. But the Germans soon invaded Holland and began rounding up all Jews to be sent to the death camps.

Her father took thirteen-year-old Anne and her mother and sister into hiding. He had a secret apartment built in his office building, and some of his employees bravely brought them food and supplies. Anne and her family hid in the cramped quarters for two years, living in constant fear of being discovered.

Anne, who had been a very good student, began to keep a journal to help pass the long days. She wrote about her family members' daily lives, about the terrible fate of their friends and others at the hands of the Nazis, and about her dreams of freedom. She still had the courage to hope.

Their secret hiding place was so well constructed that they might have stayed hidden for the entire war, but someone betrayed them and told the Nazis.

Anne's father was sent to one death camp; the two girls and their mother were sent to another. Anne's mother gave all her food to her two daughters to help keep them alive. , and starved to death; the two girls, working like slaves, sick, and existing on tiny amounts of rotten food, also died a few months later.

The only survivor was Anne's father. After the war, he went back to Holland and found the loyal workers who had hidden his family. They had saved Anne's diary, hoping to return it to her.

When Anne's father saw how well written his daughter's journal was, and the powerful tale it told of suffering under the Nazis, he determined to have it published. The Diary of Anne Frank is considered one of the most important books of the twentieth century.

Today, Anne's diary is often studied in schools to demonstrate the terrible human cost of bigotry and hatred—as well as the power of hope.

Beatrice Biira

After her family was rescued
from desperate poverty by
being given a goat, young
Beatrice Biira was able to get
an education, and she became
an international advocate
and speaker in support of
education and against poverty.

It may be hard to imagine that a goat changed someone's life, but it's true. In fact, the story of Beatrice Biira shows that goats can help change the world!

Beatrice was a child living in Kisinga, a poor village in the west of Uganda, when the goat arrived. The animal was a gift from Heifer International, an aid agency that provides animals to help struggling families like Beatrice's in many countries.

Owning a goat completely changed the world for Beatrice and her family, who were desperately poor. Suddenly, they had milk to drink and improve their health, extra milk to sell and provide urgently needed money, goat droppings to use as fertilizer for growing food, and a sense of hope for the future.

The extra money also meant that her family could afford to pay for school fees, books, and a uniform, so Beatrice was able to get the most powerful possession in the world—an education. As a bright and determined girl, Beatrice was ready to take full advantage of her new opportunities, and her intelligence and willingness to work hard made her stand out among the students.

Meanwhile, Heifer International saw what a huge difference their help had made and decided to use Beatrice Biira's story to encourage people to support their program. They created a book entitled Beatrice's Goat to explain how just one goat, cow, or other farm animal can rescue a family from poverty. The book was so popular that they invited Biira to go to the United States and tell her story to the public and the media. Wherever she went, she touched people's hearts and earned their admiration.

With the support of a scholarship, Beatrice Biira went on to attend Connecticut College, earning a BA in International Development and Social Change. As of this writing, she is working toward an MA in Public Service from the Clinton School of Public Service.

Biira is the outreach coordinator for Millennium Promise and Connect To Learn. She mobilizes and energizes communities on behalf of global campaigns to end extreme poverty in our lifetime, and to educate girls and boys through high-tech platforms.

Beatrice Biira's life was transformed by her opportunity to get an education, and that was made possible by the gift of a goat. She is now changing the lives of others in poverty.

Beatrix Potter

Storyteller, illustrator, nature lover, and self-taught nature expert, Beatrix Potter went from leading an extremely isolated life to becoming a famous and wealthy writer and illustrator of children's books.

If Beatrix Potter's parents had let her go to university, as she so badly wanted to do, she might be remembered today as one of the world's great experts on mushrooms. Instead, she became one of the bestselling children's authors of all time.

Beatrix's family was wealthy, but very strict with their daughter. She was raised away from other children, with private tutors teaching her at remote country estates in England. Her parents were determined to keep her at home for the rest of her life, to be their housekeeper and care for them in their old age.

But Beatrix had dreams. She loved nature and all plants and animals, particularly rabbits, and kept many kinds of creatures as pets. She was also an excellent artist who could create detailed and realistic paintings and drawings. Above all, Beatrix had a great imagination, and loved to read and tell stories.

Living such an isolated life, Beatrix became a nature expert, particularly with regard to plants and fungi. With her great artistic talents, she could draw amazing illustrations of mushrooms that earned her respect among naturalists.

The young woman thought she might have a future as a botanist, studying plants, but her parents wouldn't let her pursue a career, and few scientists in the 1800s would have ever taken a woman seriously.

Beatrix felt trapped in her parents' life until someone pointed a way out. Beatrix had written letters to her last governess's five-year-old son. In the letters, Beatrix had made up adventure stories about rabbits and other creatures that she loved.

The former governess thought the stories were wonderful, and encouraged Beatrix to turn them into a children's book. Writing the story and doing her own illustrations, Beatrix Potter created The Tale of Peter Rabbit. Although one publisher after another turned the idea down, Potter would not give up her dream of achievement and independence.

After years of trying, The Tale of Peter Rabbit was finally published. It was a big hit, and so were the books that followed. Characters like Squirrel Nutkin, Jemima Puddle-Duck, and the Flopsy Bunnies became favorites for children across England.

Potter earned enough money to leave home and live her own life. She married, bought a huge farm, and raised as many animals as she liked. Her more than twenty popular children's books made her wealthy and famous, but it was her hard-earned independence that Beatrix Potter treasured most.

Benjamin Franklin

Known for both his self-discipline and his sense of humor, Benjamin Franklin was famous for his many accomplishments, including his inventions.

Printer, inventor, scientist, writer, politician, and ambassador—Benjamin Franklin was all of these and more. He invented things we still use today, and changed the history of his nation. How did he do it? By being self-disciplined, he said. Ben Franklin actually set out to make himself a better person, and his efforts seemed to work.

Ben was born in the United States when it was still a British colony. He was a clever boy with a sense of humor; he used to write anonymous letters to his brother's newspaper that were so funny and biting that everyone wondered who the author could be.

Young Ben was determined to be a success. He made himself a list of good character traits he thought would help him succeed, and he practiced each one for a week at a time.

His list was: temperance (not eating or drinking too much); silence (only saying what is useful); order (keeping things in their places and doing things at the right time); resolution (always keeping your word); frugality (not wasting money); industry (working hard and making good use of your time); sincerity (not being hurtful or lying); justice (doing what's right); moderation (not too much of anything); cleanliness (body, clothes, and house); tranquility (staying calm when things go wrong); chastity (being pure with sex); and humility (not bragging).

Ben Franklin's self-discipline helped him to become a successful printer with his own newspaper and popular magazine. He became well known for sayings that are still repeated today, such as: "Honesty is the best policy"; "Time is money"; and "A penny saved is a penny earned."

Many of his inventions are also still used today—bifocal glasses, swim fins, and the Franklin wood stove, for example. He studied science, and became world-famous for his experiments that helped prove that lightning carried electricity.

Franklin was well known for his charitable work—creating a library, a fire department, and a public insurance company. He also got involved in politics, fought for American independence, and represented the United States in England and France. Back home, he helped to write the U.S. Constitution.

But, of all these accomplishments, Ben Franklin was most proud of one thing: improving himself every day.

Bertha Wilson

Not only did Bertha Wilson become the first woman to serve on the Supreme Court of Canada, she also had the courage to make groundbreaking judgments, particularly regarding women's rights.

It can be very hard to be the first one to do something—to break through a barrier and stand out from everyone else.

Bertha Wilson faced that kind of challenge when she became the first woman to serve on the Supreme Court of Canada. She became one of Canada's top judges in 1982, and to her surprise, the Court didn't even have a women's washroom!

Plenty of people thought that Wilson would not be able to handle the job because she was a woman. It didn't help that she was a soft-spoken person with a charming Scottish accent and a reserved manner. How could someone like that be tough enough for the Supreme Court? But Bertha Wilson had been a top-notch lawyer and the first woman on the Ontario Court of Appeal. Underneath her quiet demeanor, she had a brilliant mind and a strong will.

After all, Wilson, who came from a small, working-class town in Scotland, had worked her way up to one of the top law firms in Canada, fighting sexism all the way. When she had first tried to enroll in law school, the dean had told her to "Go home and take up crocheting."

So, Wilson had earned her way to the Supreme Court by being just as smart and tough as any man.

Soon, she was making the other Supreme Court justices—and the whole country—sit up and take notice. She dared to make groundbreaking judgments on issues that no one else had dared to touch, especially those regarding women's rights. Her rulings challenged the way that the law treated women in Canada.

When she died in 2007, a newspaper article commented that Bertha Wilson "delivered the news Canadians weren't always ready to hear." Her inner strength gave her the confidence to say what needed to be said, even when it was not easy or pleasant.

Thanks to her belief in herself and in her principles, Wilson proved that women could serve well in any court, at any level. Today, she gets credit for breaking the barrier and making it possible for other women to reach the highest levels of the legal profession.

Beverley McLachlin

As a lawyer, judge, and professor, and the first woman to be chief justice of the Supreme Court of British Columbia, Beverley McLachlin has dedicated her life to the idea of equal justice for all people.

There was not much doubt that Beverley McLachlin was going to be a success. Growing up in the small town of Pincher Creek, Alberta in the 1940s, Beverley was an excellent student and had learned the value of hard work from her farmer parents.

The question was—what would she do with her excellent brain? Beverley herself was not sure, even while she was going to university, but two things happened that changed her life.

The first incident was a chance meeting with a stranger on the bus. The stranger was a Native Canadian, who told Beverley how she had been taken from her family, forced to go to a "residential school," and how her culture and language were taken away from her.

The second incident was a special privilege— being chosen to go on a foreign study trip as part of one of her university programs. In the African country of Algeria, Beverley saw real poverty and injustice. She learned how hard life was for people who had no rights and no one to stand up for them.

These events strengthened Beverley McLachlin's sense of justice and fairness, and she never forgot them. She went on to earn her law degree and dedicate her life to the idea of equal justice for all people.

She soon earned a reputation as a brilliant legal mind who could tackle the trickiest situations. Within a few years, she was taking on major cases at a top law firm in Vancouver and teaching law at university.

McLachlin was a natural choice to become a judge—fair-minded and compassionate, but also tough and smart. It did not take long for her to be promoted to higher courts. She became the first woman to be chief justice of the Supreme Court of B.C., and then, in 1989, she was asked to serve in the highest court of the land, the Supreme Court of Canada.

As a judge, Beverley McLachlin has made major decisions that affect her whole nation—helping to draw the line between the rights of individuals and the power of government. Legal experts say she brings a unique and powerful point of view, coming up with solutions others might never have thought of.

But all of her decisions, and all of her work for groups dedicated to education and justice, are based on her core belief that all people deserve equal freedom, justice, and protection.

Celine Dion

Celine Dion's story proves that you never know where life will take you, even when you're one of fourteen children from a poor family. Celine is one of the most popular singers the world has ever produced, and is a multi-million dollar contributor to charities.

As the best-selling female pop singer of all time—with some 200 million albums sold—and one of the richest women in the world of entertainment, you might think that Celine Dion has had an easy life.

In fact, along with the gold records and successful world tours, her life has had many challenges, both in her childhood and during the days of her superstardom.

As the youngest of fourteen children in a poor Quebec family, Celine learned the value of a dollar from an early age. Her huge family provided her with love, encouragement, and a devotion to music, but all of the children had to pitch in to make ends meet financially.

Beginning with a homemade audio tape she made at age twelve, her career as a singer and songwriter first blossomed in her native province. Celine then had to work hard to learn English and perfect her show-business skills before she could break into the broader world music market.

In 1989, at the beginning of her career, Celine Dion nearly lost her famously powerful voice for good! She injured her voice box during a concert and was told she might need surgery to ever speak properly again. It took weeks of rest, therapy, and a new regimen of practice and technique before Dion regained her abilities.

Ten years later, she was at the height of her popularity, with gold records in both English and French covering her walls. Songs like "My Heart Will Go On" (used in the hit movie Titanic) made her a global success. But, Dion had not been able to have the one thing she wanted most—a child. And then, her husband was diagnosed with cancer.

Dion made the decision to take time off from her career. She focused on her family, nursing her husband back to health, and undergoing fertility treatments so that she could have a child. Her first child, a son, was born in 2001. She then successfully restarted her career, producing more albums and a series of sold-out shows in Las Vegas.

Today, she still reigns as the biggest music star Canada has ever produced, and one of the most popular singers in world history. As a Goodwill Ambassador for the United Nations, and a multi-million dollar contributor to health and education charities, Celine Dion helps others overcome their life challenges. In 2010, she gave birth to twin boys.

Christopher Columbus

As a sailor, sea captain, trader, and explorer, what Christopher Columbus lacked in navigation tools, he made up for with courage, daring, and perseverance as he headed straight west across an unknown ocean.

A lot of people think that Christopher Columbus "discovered" America. However, by the time he made his first voyage, in 1492, aboriginal peoples had been living in North America for tens of thousands of years. Even the Vikings, who were also Europeans, had landed in Canada hundreds of years before Columbus was born. Furthermore, Columbus himself never actually set foot on mainland North America, but landed in the Caribbean Islands.

Overall, Columbus was wrong about where he was going (Asia), how long the journey was (he thought it was 3,700 km, but it was more than 19,000 km), and where he landed (aboriginal American people became known as "Indians" because Columbus thought he had landed in India).

So, why is Columbus the most famous explorer of all time?

Partly because what Columbus accomplished was amazing for the time. In those days, Europeans trading with Asia had to sail all the way south around the tip of Africa, then east across the Indian Ocean. Columbus had the daring idea to take a short cut—straight west across the empty ocean, into the complete unknown.

It took tremendous determination for a man who was known as a trader—not an explorer—to get backing for his plan to sail around the world. The experts said it couldn't be done. One country after another turned him down until, after years of effort, Columbus finally got the king and queen of Spain to give him the money, ships, and sailors he needed.

For Columbus to sail further out of sight of land than anyone ever had done before, trusting in his own calculations and abilities, took a lot of courage. And he would need all of his seafaring abilities to find a safe route home again, using the Trade Winds that blow east across the Atlantic Ocean.

While Columbus remained convinced to his death that he had found a route to India, his voyages changed the course of history. Even with all his mix-ups, Columbus brought back to Europe the news of amazing new lands and peoples. His discovery was the start of a huge movement of Europeans who came to North, Central, and South America to explore, trade, conquer, and occupy.

Ultimately, Columbus's adventuring meant that many changes would take place in the Americas. Whether you believe those changes were good, bad, or a mix of the two, there can be no doubt that Christopher Columbus altered the world through his vision and determination.

Craig Kielburger

Creator of Free The Children, an organization whose purpose is to free child slaves all over the world and provide them with an education, Craig Kielburger was a child himself when his passion to help children began.

One morning in 1995, twelve-year-old Craig Kielburger was flipping through a newspaper, looking for the comics, and he happened to see a headline about the murder of a boy named Iqbal who was about Craig's own age.

Craig read about how Iqbal had been sold into slavery in South Asia at the age of four and spent six years chained to a carpet-making machine, working day and night. Iqbal had escaped, told his story to the world, and started fighting against child slavery.

Now, the story said, Iqbal had been killed to stop his campaign for freedom.

That terrible story touched something in Craig, and he determined to pick up Iqbal's cause and work to free children from slavery, poverty, and ignorance. It was a big ambition for a twelve-year-old, but Craig says Iqbal's story proved that the bravest voice could live in the smallest body.

So, Craig cut the article out of the paper, took it to his school in Thornhill, Ontario, and asked his classmates if they wanted to help. Eleven other kids put their hands up . . . and that was the start of the group Craig called "Free The Children."

Together, they set out to raise funds, tell people about the plight of child slaves worldwide, and—above all—to help those children get the freedom and education they needed.

Craig's friends told other friends, parents, teachers . . . the word spread quickly and Free The Children grew by leaps and bounds. Soon, they were working with other groups in third world countries, getting support from companies and associations, and creating their own education and development programs.

Today, Free The Children is the world's largest network of children helping children through education. There are more than one million youth involved in forty-five countries worldwide. They build schools, provide clean water and health care, and fight against the abuse and neglect of children . . . everything to make life better for other children and youth.

Craig Kielburger is now a grown man, but continues to dedicate his entire life to the cause he started when he was twelve. He flies all over the world, giving speeches and working with various groups that share his passion for justice. Here at home, he helps organize and support student leaders and others who want to change the world for the better.

And it all happened because Kielburger saw something disturbing in the newspaper, and refused to just turn the page.

Diane Warren

A prolific songwriter with six Oscar nominations, a Golden Globe, and Songwriter of the Year awards, Diane Warren has created a foundation that supports music programs in financially challenged schools.

Many young people feel the same way that Diane Warren did as a girl—misunderstood and somehow different from everyone around her. Growing up in California, she wanted to rebel against her parents and everything else in her world. She ran away from home as a teenager, and only came back because she missed her cat!

The truth was that Diane was different. She had a strong creative spark, and a great way with words. And she found comfort in writing songs that expressed her feelings.

While her mother thought Diane was a dreamer who should focus on getting a job as a secretary, her father encouraged her hopes of becoming a song-writer. With that encouragement and a strong will to follow her own direction in life, Diane began the tough task of trying to sell her songs.

Her determination and talent paid off with her first hit song in the 1980s—"Solitaire," performed by Laura Branigan. Other hits quickly followed—pop hits, rock hits, country hits—performed by some of the biggest names in music, including Celine Dion, Trisha Yearwood, Toni Braxton, and LeAnn Rimes.

Warren's career soared to new heights when her songs began to appear in hit films, resulting in six Oscar nominations and a Golden Globe award for "You Haven't Seen the Last of Me," performed by Cher in the movie Burlesque. She now has a star on the celebrated Hollywood Walk of Fame and has been named Songwriter of the Year six times, among a host of other honors and awards.

But Diane Warren did not forget what it felt like to be that lonely girl with a love for music. She has used her fame and fortune to start a foundation that supports music programs in financially challenged schools, and she helps sponsor contests for emerging songwriters.

Recalling how her father was the one person to encourage her love of music, she wrote the hit song "Because You Loved Me" as a tribute to his support.

In 1993, the struggling Montreal Canadiens adopted one of Diane Warren's songs, "Nothing's Gonna Stop Us Now," as their unofficial anthem, and went on to win the Stanley Cup that year. Just like Warren herself, they demonstrated the power of determination and self-belief.

Eleanor Roosevelt

As wife of a politician who became president of the United States, Eleanor Roosevelt used her high profile and spirited personality to become a renowned international activist, speaker, and author.

Eleanor Roosevelt was born into privilege and wealth. Her family had plenty of money and was part of New York high society, and her uncle Teddy was president of the United States.

But Eleanor's early life was hard; her mother and brother both died of illness when she was very young, and her father drank himself to death. She was a lonely, quiet, shy girl with no confidence, despite the fact that she was very intelligent.

It was only as a teenager that Eleanor began to blossom. She started doing well in school, volunteered to do social work in the poor neighborhoods of New York, and began to believe in herself. Even though she knew that she was no great beauty, Eleanor decided that honesty and loyalty would show in her face and make her attractive from the inside out.

It seems she was right—she attracted the attention of a distant relative named Franklin, a tall, handsome man who seemed destined for great things in politics. But again, fate set out a hard road for Eleanor Roosevelt. Her husband had an affair, then developed polio and was very ill for a long time.

This is when Eleanor Roosevelt's real character came out, and her determination and spirit only grew stronger. She began to be a force in politics herself, stepping in for her sick husband in public appearances while getting him back on his feet again at home.

Thanks in large part to Eleanor, Franklin won the election to become governor of New York State and then, in 1933, to become president of the United States of America. Eleanor Roosevelt now had a very high profile.

From then on, this remarkable woman used her fame and dynamic personality to fight for every cause she believed in. She was a great supporter of equality for women and minorities, helped form the United Nations and write its Declaration of Human Rights, and won praise from soldiers for her compassionate visits to the front lines in World War II.

As an international author, speaker, and activist, she was a role model for women around the world at a time when few women had such public roles. Eleanor Roosevelt encouraged all people, whatever their gender or race, to live up to their potentials and pursue their dreams, just as she had done.

Today, polls in the United States still rank her as one of the most admired Americans in history.

Ferdinand Magellan

A sixteenth-century seaman, trader, fighter, and explorer, Ferdinand Magellan was captain of the fleet that took on the high-risk challenge of circumnavigating the globe.

In the 1500s, Spain and Portugal were global power-houses and bitter rivals. Both nations were experts at exploring and trading by sea, and at fighting over the riches they found.

It was an opportune time for a man like Ferdinand Magellan—an expert sailor and even better fighter. He took part in many voyages and battles for his native Portugal, earning a stellar reputation.

Magellan came up with a visionary plan to put his nation on top in the ongoing rivalry with Spain: Instead of sailing all the way around Africa to get to the trading lands of Asia, why not go the other way around the world?

Magellan thought if he could find a way past the new lands where Christopher Columbus had landed in Central and South America, he could open up fresh trade routes. By doing this, he imagined, he could make his country—and himself—rich!

But the king of Portugal had just signed a treaty giving him power over the standard trade route around Africa. He wasn't interested in a risky expedition into the unknown. Even worse, Magellan's enemies at court were spreading false stories, and the king stopped trusting him.

There was one risky step that Magellan could

take to keep his dream alive: he could go to Spain. The Spanish suspected Magellan of being a spy. But the Spanish king was desperate to find a new path to Asia, and he took the chance of backing Magellan's daring scheme.

Now all Ferdinand Magellan had to do was sail across the two biggest oceans on Earth, through uncharted waters, to the other side of the world!

Magellan set out with high hopes. But shipwrecks, mutiny, disease, attacks by native tribes, powerful storms, and other disasters plagued him all along the way. Finally, after weeks of hitting dead ends as he attempted to round the tip of South America, Ferdinand Magellan found a way through and sailed his battered fleet to success.

Much later, Magellan got caught up in a civil war in the Philippines and was killed in battle. His deputy decided to press on, through Asian waters, around Africa, and back to Spain. The sailors who survived became the first people to sail around the world!

Only eighteen sailors and one leaky boat from the fleet of 250 men and five ships made it home. But, they proved Ferdinand Magellan had been right. Today, the route around South America is called the Strait of Magellan after one of the bravest, most determined explorers in history.

Florence Nightingale

Eschewing the upper-class British life into which she'd been born, Florence Nightingale became a nurse on the front lines of war, advocated for improved sanitation in hospitals, and started the world's first official training program for nurses.

A woman born into a wealthy, upper-class British home in the early 1800s was supposed to do just one thing: become the wife of a wealthy, upper-class man.

But, Florence Nightingale had other ideas. Her father had taught her advanced mathematics, so young Florence knew she had a good brain. To Florence, the comfortable lives of the wealthy women around her seemed shallow. She felt she was destined for something more worthwhile.

At age seventeen, Florence announced that she had found her calling in life—she wanted to become a nurse. Her mother and sister were horrified. Wealthy young women of that time simply did not work, and certainly avoided all contact with "the lower classes."

It took a lot of strength of character for Nightingale to go against the conventions of the day and the wishes of her family. But she persisted, working hard to study nursing, and traveling around Europe and the Middle East to broaden her education.

Other wealthy English people thought she was eccentric or shameful, but the Crimean War changed everything and made Florence Nightingale a national heroine.

The war involving the British, Russian, French, and Ottoman empires created terrible conditions for wounded soldiers. There was little medicine, a scarcity of trained doctors, and virtually no sanitation. More soldiers were dying of diseases in the hospitals than were being killed on the battlefield.

Florence Nightingale led a group of volunteer nurses to the front lines in what is now Turkey. The soldiers there described her as an "angel," and nicknamed her The Lady with the Lamp due to her late-night visits to comfort the sick and dying. The story of this wealthy woman who put aside riches and comfort to risk her life in filthy conditions became a national sensation in Britain, and inspired many people to follow her example.

After the war, Florence Nightingale used her skills in advanced mathematics to determine why so many soldiers had died. She realized that sanitation was the key to saving lives, and began to campaign for cleaner conditions in hospitals. She invented a new kind of pie chart, the "Nightingale Rose Diagram," to prove her point to politicians and bureaucrats who didn't understand statistics.

Florence Nightingale took advantage of her newly acquired fame to raise funds and set up the world's first official training program for nurses. She is considered the founder of modern nursing.

Galileo Galilei

An astronomer, mathematician, inventor, and author, Galileo Galilei was a rebel genius in the 1600s who was sentenced as a heretic by the Catholic Church.

He's been called the father of modern astronomy, the father of modern physics, even the father of all modern science, but Galileo Galilei (who is known by his first name only) was a rebel. He did not set out to turn the science world and the Roman Catholic Church on their collective ears, but that's what happened.

The son of a musician in Italy, Galileo was a naturally curious man with a great gift for mathematics and invention. When someone told him that a scientist in Holland thought it might be possible to use a tube with glass lenses to see far away, Galileo sat down and built the first modern telescope.

Sea captains and others loved his invention, but it was when Galileo turned one of his telescopes towards the sky that he began to get into trouble.

In the Europe of the early 1600s, the Catholic Church was the ultimate power. People who questioned its version of the world risked being labeled "heretics," and arrested, tortured, even killed. The Church insisted that the Earth was the center of the universe and that the planets were perfect spheres, and anyone who tried to contradict these ideas was in great danger. The problem was that Galileo's telescope had shown him that the Church's teachings on this matters was wrong.

Galileo proved that the Earth orbited around the Sun, not the other way around. He found moons orbiting Jupiter and Saturn, when the Church said everything was supposed to revolve around the Earth. And Galileo even measured the mountains and valleys on the Moon, showing that it was not the perfect sphere the Church claimed it to be.

Galileo not only made these discoveries, he also published them in widely popular books that often made fun of the ignorance of his critics. Even though he tried to tiptoe around the Church's positions, everything Galileo did proved them wrong.

It was only a matter of time before Galileo was put on trial and sentenced as a heretic. He spent the rest of his life under house arrest, and all of his books were banned.

A true scientist to the end, Galileo kept experimenting and writing in secret, even as an old man. It was only long after his death, when there was so much proof that his findings could no longer be ignored, that Galileo's work was fully recognized. In 1992, the Catholic Church apologized and admitted he had been right.

Gordon Lightfoot

Singer, songwriter, and winner of sixteen Juno awards, Gordon Lightfoot is still writing and performing after more than fifty years in the business.

Looking at Gordon Lightfoot's music career, you might assume his life has been a breeze. After all, his singing talent was recognized when he was still a little boy in Orillia, Ontario, and he was already appearing on stage, radio, and television when he was a teenager.

Throughout the 1960s and 70s, Lightfoot had a string of hit songs (recorded by himself and other top stars who loved his song writing), and he broke records with his sold-out concerts at Toronto's Massey Hall.

However, behind the scenes, Lightfoot struggled. In 1972, at the height of his popularity, he suffered a serious illness—Bell's palsy—that paralyzed part of his face. For a singer and performer, this was a serious threat to his career. He fought his way through the illness and regained his health, even while keeping up a heavy recording and touring schedule.

For the next thirty years, Gordon Lightfoot continued to record albums, perform concerts, and appear on television. By 2002, he was no longer a superstar with number one hits, but he still had legions of fans and his performances attracted huge crowds.

Then, tragedy struck again during a tour in his hometown, when a major artery in Lightfoot's stomach suddenly burst. He was airlifted to a hospital by helicopter for emergency treatment to save his life. It took five operations and a three-month hospital stay to get him out of danger.

Gordon Lightfoot refused to give up his life as an entertainer. Against all odds, he made a comeback and by 2004, he was recording and touring again. Even a stroke he suffered in 2007 that cost him the use of some of his fingers could not hold him back. Lightfoot practiced tirelessly until he could play the guitar again, and then went back on the road.

After a music career of more than fifty years, Gordon Lightfoot is a member of several music halls of fame, winner of sixteen Juno Awards, and a Companion of the Order of Canada. With more than 200 recordings to his credit, including several gold records, his fellow musicians consider him a songwriting legend.

Gordon Lightfoot has nothing left to prove, but he has an unending passion for writing and performing his music. As of 2011, at age seventy-two, he is still recording and touring.

Grandma Moses

Although Grandma Moses didn't pick up a paint brush until she was seventy, she still had time to become world famous, with shows in the U.S., Europe, and Asia. She continued painting for more than thirty years.

Very few artists are able to make a living from their art. Even fewer become famous around the world, set attendance records when their work is displayed, and have their paintings hanging everywhere from the White House to European and Asian museums. Only one artist has ever done all of that, despite the fact that she had no training and didn't even start painting until she was more than seventy years old!

The incredible story of Anna "Grandma" Moses sounds like a corny movie plot, but it's all true.

The mother of ten children, Moses was a very active grandmother and great-grandmother, known in the little town of Hoosick Falls, New York for doing lovely embroidery. But arthritis was making it more difficult for her to do her needlework, and she wanted to make a Christmas gift for her postman. Moses decided to try painting him a picture instead.

The postman loved his painting, and Moses found that she enjoyed working with paint and canvas. Soon she was painting all the time, and giving her artwork away to friends and relatives.

Anna Moses's paintings were so charming that other people wanted to buy them, so the woman who was about to take the art world by storm started selling her paintings for two to three dollars each.

Then, when Moses was seventy-eight years old, the miracle happened. In 1938, an art collector just happened to be passing through Hoosick Falls and saw some of her paintings for sale in the local drug store. He bought every one, tracked Anna Moses down, and then he bought every painting she had at home, too!

Within a year, three of her paintings were included in a show at the famous Museum of Modern Art in New York City. Galleries and collectors started talking about this amazing new artist who captured rural scenes and people in a delightful folk-art style.

It didn't take long for Grandma Moses, as everyone called her, to become famous. Shows of her work were staged in major galleries and museums across the United States, and then in Europe and Asia. Everywhere that her paintings were shown, record crowds came out to see them and buy them.

Grandmas Moses took it all in stride. She said that starting a new career in your seventies and being active in your nineties just required a positive attitude.

Anna Moses kept painting right up to her death at age 101, producing more than 3,600 paintings.

Gustavo Dudamel

World-famous conductor Gustavo Dudamel, "the lightning conductor", can turn a solid old symphony into "molten lava." Today, he plans to recreate the successful youth orchestra program for street youth that helped him.

When it comes to classical music, Gustavo Dudamel is a total rock star. At age thirty, he was (by far) the youngest conductor of a major orchestra anywhere in the world. With his wild hair, all-consuming passion, and lively sense of humor, he is also one of the most popular.

Gustavo was a musical genius as a child, and began winning international conducting prizes when he was barely out of high school. But what has always been extraordinary about Gustavo Dudamel is not only his talent, but the way he has chosen to use that gift to improve the world.

As of this writing, as well as being in his twelfth year as music director of the Venezuelan Simón Bolívar Youth Orchestra, Dudamel is also in his second season as music director of the Los Angeles Philharmonic Orchestra. With his global reputation, he could have chosen to work with any orchestra in the world, but he chose the Los Angeles Philharmonic: and he did it for a very specific reason.

Dudamel, who came from a musical family in Venezuela, had his talent recognized and supported by "El Sistema" (The System)—a revolutionary music-training program in his home country that introduces poor kids, some of them street kids, to the discipline and self-esteem of great musicianship. Recognizing how The System changed his life, Dudamel decided to introduce the program to the United States, and the hard streets of Los Angeles were a perfect place to start. So, as part of his contract with the Los Angeles Philharmonic, Gustavo Dudamel insisted on being given the money and time to start a youth orchestra.

The Youth Orchestra of Los Angeles gives poor and street youth a new focus in their lives and a new sense of accomplishment as they play to sold-out audiences at venues like the famous Hollywood Bowl. As well, Dudamel's vision of spreading the idea across the U.S. is beginning to be realized, with new community and city youth orchestras being formed in several American cities.

Dudamel's long-term dream is to see The System become as popular in other countries as it is in Venezuela, where 600 youth orchestras help a quarter of a million children stay out of trouble, develop self-discipline, and learn to believe in themselves.

Gustavo Dudamel knows firsthand that music can help change the lives of children and youth, and improve the society they live in.

Hayley Wickenheiser

An amazing, record-breaking female hockey player, Hayley Wickenheiser's love of hockey started when she was a young girl. She proved to be not only passionate, but also highly skilled, determined, and tough.

There's no doubt that Hayley Wickenheiser is the greatest female hockey player in the world.

The list of her accomplishments is remarkable. She is the first woman ever to play full-time professional hockey (other than as goalie). She has won three Olympic gold medals and a silver, and six golds and three silvers at the World Championships. You could fill pages with all of her awards, medals, and records. But all of this glory did not come easily.

Hayley's love of hockey started when she was just a few years old: as she was learning to skate she was already dreaming of becoming a hockey player. Hayley not only had a knack for skating, she also had the spirit to keep practicing and keep pushing herself to improve.

Even with her remarkable natural talent, Hayley faced many challenges growing up as a female hockey player in rural Saskatchewan. She played on boys' teams until she was thirteen, and had to prove over and over that she was just as good, or better, than her teammates.

Hayley's formula for success was simple: she just worked harder than anyone else did. Her dedication made her not only an award-winning player, but also an inspiring role model for other girls.

After becoming a star in women's amateur hockey and international tournaments, Hayley Wickenheiser turned her eyes toward the biggest prize yet—the professional leagues, where only men played.

She made her historic breakthrough in professional leagues in Europe. Again, she had to out-work the men around her to be fast enough and strong enough to hold her own. Playing there in 2003, Wickenheiser added another remarkable credit to her career—becoming the first woman to score a professional hockey goal.

Back home in Canada, she is a national hero—captain of the Olympic and national hockey teams, top goal scorer, most valuable player, and regular member of all-star squads.

But it's not just her accomplishments that make her a star—it's also her attitude. Sports Illustrated magazine has named Hayley Wickenheiser one of the "Twenty-Five Toughest Athletes Ever." She's living proof of how hard work and determination, combined with talent, can make you the best in the world.

Hazel McCallion

Not only has Hazel McCallion been the highly popular mayor of Mississauga for an unheard-of thirty-three years, in the most recent election, she received more than seventy-five percent of the votes.

A lot of things have changed in Mississauga, Ontario since 1978. It has grown from a collection of small towns and villages to the sixth-largest city in Canada. But one thing has not changed since 1978—Hazel McCallion is still the mayor! After more than three decades, she is one of the longest-serving and most popular politicians Canada has ever known.

Hazel was born to a poor family in rural Quebec that couldn't afford to send their bright daughter to university. She became a secretary instead, determined to earn her own way. Hazel didn't mind hard work and was ready to make the best of any challenge.

After being transferred to a job in Toronto, Hazel married a man she'd met at church, and one of their wedding presents changed her life—and Canadian politics—forever. The present was a small plot of land in a little town called Streetsville, not far from Toronto.

At the time that Hazel McCallion and her husband settled in Streetsville, the area was growing rapidly. Together, they started a small newspaper and became involved in local issues. It wasn't long before McCallion, with her keen mind and tremendous energy, was a real force in local politics. By the time that Streetsville and other towns in the area were put together to form the new city of Mississauga, Hazel McCallion was ready to run for mayor.

She not only won that first election, she has won every single election since—a remarkable string of twelve consecutive elections. McCallion became so popular that she really didn't need to campaign, and she asked people to donate money to charity rather than to her election fund!

Running the city—in her words—"like a business" has made Mississauga one of the few debt-free cities in Canada. Her effective management and plainspoken style has kept voters loyal to her for over thirty-three years. In the most recent election—in 2010—she received more than three quarters of the votes.

Over the years, McCallion has been called a heroine for her roles in safely evacuating the city after a massive train derailment and explosion in 1979, for talking down an armed man in 2006, and for her relentless work in getting more funding and jobs for her city.

While her strong personality has at times gotten her into trouble and earned her the nickname "Hurricane Hazel," the Mississauga mayor has also been honored with the Order of Canada and voted as one of the top mayors in the world.

Helen Keller

Although blind and deaf,
Helen Keller became a scholar,
author, speaker, advocate
for social justice, and one of
the founders of the American
Civil Liberties Union.

We all admire those who go on to lead productive lives after being struck blind or deaf in early life—but what can we say about Helen Keller, who was left both blind and deaf after a childhood illness, but went on to become one of the most famous writers, activists, and public speakers of her day?

Helen Keller was born in 1880, long before the arrival of the technology and training that can help blind and deaf people today. She was trapped in a private world, unable to communicate or understand the world around her.

Helen's family turned to an expert on helping the deaf—Alexander Graham Bell, the inventor of the telephone. He recommended a special school where highly trained teachers could be hired to help girls like Helen. And that's how Anne Sullivan came into Helen's life.

Sullivan began to teach Helen words by tracing symbols on the girl's hand. Helen didn't understand at first, but one day when Sullivan poured some water on Helen's hand and then traced the letters for "water," the young girl made the connection.

That's when Helen's remarkable brain and determination kicked in. Once she realized that there was a way of communicating with others, she learned at an incredible rate. From simple words to complicated ideas, Helen Keller absorbed knowledge like a sponge.

Accompanied by the loyal Anne Sullivan, Keller went to school and soon excelled as a student. She was even accepted by a top university and became the first deaf and blind person to ever earn a bachelor of arts degree. But that was just the start. She was now reading Braille in several languages, and became very interested in politics and social issues. Despite her challenges, Keller set out to make a difference in the world.

Soon she was deeply involved in many issues—voting rights for women, better treatment for the disabled, anti-war campaigns, and social justice. She wrote salient letters to newspapers, gave rousing speeches, wrote bestselling books, came up with all kinds of ideas and slogans, and even helped found the American Civil Liberties Union (ACLU). She was like a whirlwind!

Helen Keller's brilliant mind and inspiring story won her many fans and a high profile worldwide. She was friends with people like author Mark Twain, and met with every American president who served during her lifetime.

Above all, she inspired others not to let physical challenges stand in the way of achieving their full potentials.

J. K. Rowling

J. K. Rowling planned out her
entire book series before she
started writing the first one—
by hand. Twelve publishers are
probably still cursing because
they rejected her first Harry
Potter book, convinced it
was far too long for children
and would never sell.

She is worth more than a billion dollars, has been named one of the most influential people in the world, and holds the record for the fastest-selling books in history. But when J. K. Rowling first set out to write her books about a boy wizard named Harry Potter, no one could possibly have guessed how successful she would be. In fact, Joanne Rowling (her real name) was having a hard time, and had to fight against tremendous odds to achieve her vision.

Rowling says she came up with the Harry Potter idea while riding on a train that was delayed. By the time it got to the station, she had the whole series of books plotted out in her mind!

She started writing right away, but then life threw her a series of curves. Following the death of her mother after a long battle with multiple sclerosis, Rowling took a job teaching in Portugal. She got married and had a baby there, but after a divorce she moved back to Britain.

Three years later, she still had not finished her first Harry Potter book. She was a single, unemployed mother, living on welfare. But J. K. Rowling still believed in her idea. She would take her baby for long walks to put her to sleep, and then sit writing her book in cafes. She finally finished the manuscript and typed it up on an old manual typewriter.

The first twelve publishers turned her down. Number thirteen said, "Yes"—mainly because the little girl of the company's chairperson loved the book— but warned Rowling to get a job because she would not make much money from a children's book.

Once Harry Potter and the Philosopher's Stone was published, however, the book won a raft of awards and began selling at an incredible pace. Every book in the series sold more than the last, with the last four books all setting world records for the fastest sale of a million copies.

All told, the Harry Potter series has sold 400 million copies in sixty-five languages, sparked a series of highly successful movies, and made J. K. Rowling one of the wealthiest authors in the world.

Rowling remembers her own struggles and gives millions of dollars a year to charities, including those that focus on poverty and on multiple sclerosis. She is also president of a charity that supports single parents.

Jacques Cousteau

Famous for his award-winning underwater films, television shows, and books that gave the world a view of life under the ocean, ecologist Jacques Cousteau was also a talented inventor and dedicated environmental activist.

★ 112 ★

Naval officer, explorer, ecologist, filmmaker, innovator, scientist, photographer, author, researcher ... you could go on for pages about all of the things Jacques Cousteau did with his remarkable life!

Many people outside France don't know that Costeau was a war hero; he led daring commando operations inside occupied France during World War II. And many may not know that he helped invent the modern aqualung—the SCUBA system that's used around the world.

Most people remember Jacques Cousteau for his amazing films, television shows, and books about the ocean. On board his ship Calypso, Cousteau and his crew traveled the world to film their documentaries about the life that teems beneath the surface of the water.

In the 1950s and 60s, Cousteau's films marked the first time the majority of people had ever seen footage of undersea life in its natural state. And it was the first time that the general public heard about the dangers of pollution, overfishing, habitat destruction, and other threats to the natural world.

Jacques Cousteau is credited with being one of the first popular ecologists, inspiring a whole generation of young people to be more aware of their environment.

His long career (Cousteau lived to age eighty-seven) contained many other amazing achievements:

- The first underwater archaeology operation using autonomous diving;
- Discovering how porpoises use natural sonar to guide themselves;
- Winning the top prize at the world-famous Cannes Film Festival for his documentary The Silent World;

Organizing a successful campaign to stop the dumping of nuclear waste in the oceans; and

Winning a long list of awards and medals from grateful nations and organizations around the world.

Through more than 120 television documentaries and fifty books, Cousteau helped make science and nature popular topics for everyday people, and he left a legacy that carries on his work. The Cousteau Society he founded to protect the environment now has 300,000 members. As rich and famous as he became, Jacques Cousteau always said he was just a man trying to do his bit to help the world. "It takes generosity to discover the whole through others," he said. "If you realize you are only a violin, you can open yourself up to the world by playing your role in the concert."

Jean Vanier

Jean Vanier's belief that people with developmental disabilities should live in communities rather than in isolation from them launched an international movement— "L'Arche"—that has now spread to thirty countries.

When he was just thirteen, Jean Vanier set out to become a naval officer and could have had a very successful career. But as a young man, he felt something greater was calling him. He quit the navy and began a search for meaning in his life, believing that God had a plan for him.

As the son of one of Canada's governor generals, Vanier grew up with a life of privilege. But when he became friends with a priest in France who worked with the developmentally disabled, he was exposed to another world—a world where people were rejected, feared, or ignored because of their mental disabilities. Vanier felt God wanted him to do something to address this form of prejudice.

So Vanier bought an old farmhouse, named it L'Arche (French for Noah's Ark), and invited two developmentally disabled men to come and live with him in a real home. Without knowing it, Jean Vanier had started an international movement. There are now more than 130 L'Arche communities in thirty countries around the world.

That didn't happen overnight or by itself. Vanier traveled the globe, spreading his message that the mentally disabled would be better off living in communities instead of institutions—and that all of us would be better off if we shared our lives with people who challenge our way of thinking, and show us different perspectives.

We are all "broken" in different ways, says Vanier—meaning that we all have difficulty dealing with certain issues or seeing ourselves as we really are. He believes living with the mentally disabled helps people deal with their own issues, learn compassion, and become better human beings.

For more than forty years, Jean Vanier has crisscrossed the world to inspire others to follow his example. Besides the L'Arche communities, he has helped found other organizations to help people with developmental disabilities and their families through faith and community support, and he has written more than twenty books explaining his life and philosophy.

While Vanier has been honored by governments and popes, and has received countless awards and medals, he continues to live in the original L'Arche community in France, sharing his life with the disabled individuals and fellow volunteers he calls his friends.

John F. Kennedy

A young, dynamic, and well-loved president, JFK was passionate about ending racial discrimination in America, creating nuclear arms treaties with Russia, and landing astronauts on the moon. He was assassinated before all of his visions were realized.

"Ask not what your country can do for you—ask what you can do for your country." That was the challenge that John F. Kennedy gave to his fellow Americans after being elected president of the United States in 1960.

Kennedy came from a wealthy and influential family, and attended the finest schools. However, he was not a spoiled rich kid—he was a decorated war hero, and he became a strong and dynamic president.

One of the youngest presidents in American history, JFK (as he was often called) was handsome, vital, and full of dreams. He wanted the United States to play a bigger role in the world, particularly by encouraging democracy and fighting poverty. Kennedy spoke passionately about social justice in his own country, including an end to the ongoing racism against African-Americans. And he had to fight with members of his own party over human rights issues.

JFK also had ambitions for the entire human race, stating that he wanted to see people landing on the moon within ten years.

As president, JFK's dreams faced many challenges, not the least of which was the tension between the U.S. and Russia that came to be known as the "Cold War," leading to one crisis after another. In 1962, Kennedy faced what is known as the Cuban Missile Crisis. It was one of two major confrontations during the Cold War period, and is generally regarded as the moment in which the Cold War came closest to turning into a nuclear conflict.

As well, the United States was being drawn into the problems of Vietnam, which would lead to an unpopular war. Through it all, Kennedy continued to challenge and inspire Americans to change the world.

Then, just three years after being elected, JFK was assassinated. Americans were in shock; they could not believe their young and vital leader was dead.

In the face of tragedy, JFK's ambitious dreams lived on. He had laid the groundwork for nuclear arms treaties with Russia, civil rights legislation that banned discrimination, and the Apollo space program that in 1969 landed the first human on the moon—just as JFK had dreamed.

Although historians recognize that Kennedy had to make a lot of compromises when it came to upholding his vision and principles, Americans remember him as a great leader and a man determined to help his country achieve greatness.

Joseph Pulitzer

A journalist, investigative reporter, publisher, and advocate for freedom of the press, Joseph Pulitzer also started the first school of Journalism—at Columbia University—and created the famous Pulitzer Prizes for journalism and literature.

If Joseph Pulitzer had been born with better eyesight, or hadn't known how to play chess, our newspapers would not be the same today. When he was a teenager in Hungary in the 1860s, Joseph decided to become a soldier, but his eyesight was so bad that no army would take him. Finally, a recruiter from the United States signed him up to fight in the American Civil War.

After a year as a soldier, and having managed to survive the Civil War, Pulitzer stayed in America, working odd jobs and learning English. Then, a chance meeting changed his life and changed the world of journalism forever.

As he was studying at the library in St. Louis, he saw two men playing chess. He suggested a good move to one of them, and the three started up a conversation. The two men were publishers of a newspaper, and they offered Pulitzer a job.

Joseph Pulitzer turned out to be a brilliant and hard-working reporter. After a few years, he became publisher of the newspaper. Then, after making one smart deal after another, he wound up owning the largest newspaper in the city—the St. Louis Post-Dispatch.

That's when Pulitzer's real genius came out. He made his newspaper the voice of the common people, investigating gambling rackets, political corruption, and rich tax dodgers. People loved this new, crusading style of journalism, and circulation soared.

Joseph Pulitzer kept working hard even after he had become very ill and his eyesight was nearly gone. He believed that it was important for newspapers to serve a social purpose and help protect people from dishonesty and corruption. After a few years, he was able to buy another newspaper, this time in New York, and bring his populist approach to an even larger audience.

In 1909, his New York paper broke the story of one of the biggest political scandals in American history—$40 million in illegal payments in the Panama Canal deal. The U.S. government tried to sue him, but Pulitzer stood firm and won an important victory for freedom of the press.

Joseph Pulitzer willed part of his fortune to establish the world's first school of journalism at New York's Columbia University. He also set aside money for annual prizes for journalists and writers; today, winning one of the famous Pulitzer Prizes makes you a superstar among writers.

Although he fell into journalism by accident, Joseph Pulitzer set standards that newspapers still strive to attain today.

Laura Secord

In the early 1800s, when Laura Secord overheard American soldiers planning a sneak attack on a British/Canadian outpost, she traveled by foot through woods, fields, and rivers in enemy territory to warn the unsuspecting British and Canadian soldiers.

The United States was still a British colony when Laura Secord was born there in 1775. A year later, the United States rebelled against Britain in the War of Independence. But some Americans, like Laura's father, stayed loyal to Britain and fought against the rebels. Like many other "Loyalists," he later moved his family to Canada, where the British still ruled. They settled in the Niagara Peninsula, near Niagara Falls and the American border.

At that time, there was still a lot of tension between Canadians and Americans. Then in 1812, Britain and the United States went to war again, and this time the Americans tried to invade Canada. Laura Secord's husband was seriously wounded in one of the early battles of that war, at nearby Queenston Heights. She rushed to the battlefield, rescued him, and brought him home. That was just the first example on record of her remarkable courage.

A year later, the war was turning into a seesaw struggle, with both sides trying to control the Niagara area. The Americans had taken over Secord's neighborhood, and American officers would show up at her home demanding to be fed.

Apparently it was during one of these meals that Secord overheard them talking about their next military strategy—a surprise attack on a British/Canadian outpost twelve miles away. With her disabled husband unable to help, it was up to Secord. Did this petite, delicate-looking woman have the courage to sneak through enemy-held territory with her secret information?

It turned out that she had not only the courage, but also the smarts and determination to achieve her goal. Secord avoided American sentries on the roads by cutting through the woods, crossing rivers and fields on foot, without a map: ultimately covering more than twenty miles to reach her destination.

It took her all day and she arrived exhausted, but Laura Secord arrived in time. When the Americans attacked the next day, they didn't have a chance—the British and Canadian soldiers were waiting for them.

Laura Secord received no official thanks or recognition for her brave act until she was eighty-five years old, but today there are monuments in her honor, and history books credit her with helping Canada win the War of 1812.

Louis Braille

Blind from age three, Louis Braille
learned to read at a school for the
blind in Paris where, at that time,
books for the blind could weigh
as much as a hundred pounds!
Inspired by the indented dots
on dice, he invented the Braille
system of reading and writing.

In 1812, a three-year-old boy was playing in his father's leather workshop in Coupvray, France when he had an accident that would change the world. Louis Braille accidentally poked himself in the eye with an awl: The metal point blinded him in one eye and an infection soon left him totally blind.

Louis was a bright boy and won a scholarship to a school for the blind in Paris. It was not a particularly nice place; students were often fed bread and water and locked up for punishment. Louis and the other blind children were taught various skills (Louis became expert at playing the organ and cello), and they were taught to read. At that time, books for the blind used raised letters with metal wires under the paper, and some of the books weighed one hundred pounds!

One day, a soldier visited the school and talked about a code system that he had invented in the French army. It used raised dots and dashes on a piece of paper to allow soldiers to send each other messages in the dark while remaining silent.

Louis and the other children found the system too confusing, but the basic idea stuck in the boy's head. He began experimenting with different ways of creating a language using raised dots on paper—and for this, he used the same awl that had blinded him!

One day, Louis Braille happened to pick up a pair of dice and feel the six dots on one side. That's when inspiration struck him. He soon developed a code for each letter of the alphabet, with numbers and symbols like periods and question marks, all using no more than six dots.

One great advantage of his system was that you could read each letter or symbol using the tip of your finger. With practice, a reader could run his finger along a line and read very quickly. The other big plus was that blind people using Braille's system could write as well as read. His system opened up a whole new world!

It took many years for the Braille system to take off, and its popularity was still spreading when Louis died in 1852. Not many people can say that they invented an entire new system of reading and writing, but Louis Braille did. What's more, his system was adopted around the world, and today is available in virtually every language that humans speak.

Louis Pasteur

Louis Pasteur's germ theory was a breakthrough in medicine. He then went on to figure out how to prevent diseases by creating vaccines for cholera, smallpox, anthrax and rabies, and by developing a food-purification method called "pasteurization."

Back in the 1800s, people typically did not live long and healthy lives. Serious illness was very common, and people often died young.

French chemistry professor Louis Pasteur and his wife had five children, and three of them died in childhood of typhoid (a disease caused by drinking water tainted with bacteria). Unlike most people who simply accepted that the death of children was something that happened in most families, Pasteur made a vow to find out how illnesses like this worked, and to find a way to stop them.

At that time, there was a big debate in the medical profession about where illnesses came from: many people believed that "bad" particles just created themselves out of nowhere. Pasteur helped prove once and for all that these particles—or germs—were carried in the air and would grow and multiply where they landed.

His findings led to ideas that seemed revolutionary then, like doctors washing their hands before operating on patients! His germ theory alone would make Pasteur a great figure in science, but his work was only half done. Now that he had shown where diseases came from, he set out to discover how to prevent the diseases, and cure them.

In the course of experimenting with chickens and deliberately giving them cholera, Pasteur discovered that cholera bacteria that had been left to grow old and weak would not make the birds very sick; in fact, injections made the chickens immune to fresh cholera bacteria for the rest of their lives.

Pasteur had just invented the modern vaccine.

Louis Pasteur went on to create vaccines for other common diseases of the day, like anthrax, smallpox, and rabies. He was hailed as a hero for saving countless lives and preventing untold misery.

But Pasteur made another discovery—one that has made him a household name to this very day. He found that when milk and other foods went "bad," it was because of the bacteria and mold that had begun to grow in them. Most importantly, he proved that heating up the food would kill most of these microorganisms.

The process he developed for making food safer is called "pasteurization," and today you'll find pasteurized milk, cheese, and other products in homes around the world.

Louis Pasteur kept his vow on behalf of his children, and saved innumerable families the death and pain that his family had suffered.

Malcolm Gladwell

Malcolm Gladwell's first book, The Tipping Point, created a sensation: It contained original thinking with huge practical applications. He followed that book with others that were equally creative, and just as successful.

"Little things can make a big difference." "Trust your gut and follow your instincts." "Success usually comes down to hard work and learning from what other people have already done."

These familiar sayings are a lot more than just words to Malcolm Gladwell. He has written a number of internationally bestselling books that use science and statistics to prove why such simple sayings are true.

Gladwell, who was born in England but raised in Canada, has been a newspaper and magazine writer for many years, but his books have made him famous.

His first book, The Tipping Point, demonstrates how small ideas and trends can build up into a huge force. A catchy idea that gets out at the right time to well-connected people can literally change the world. Using concrete examples, he shows how some products and brands get to be famous, seemingly overnight, and how we can use this same method to make important social issues into the topics everyone is talking about.

In his second book, Blink, Gladwell writes about our minds, and about how quickly our subconscious is able make good decisions. In other words, our so-called "gut instincts" (the thoughts and emotions we have without consciously thinking about them) are usually reliable. He also says that if you work at learning and practicing how to do something, you can tap the power of your subconscious to do it automatically—quickly and effectively.

In his third book, Outliers, Gladwell explains that while the extraordinary people we see changing the world have often had lucky breaks, we can nevertheless achieve amazing success by taking advantage of our opportunities and simply putting in the effort. He demonstrates, through examples, that success usually comes after a long history of work by many people, each of them building on what others have done before—and he points out that we can all be part of that chain.

Malcolm Gladwell wants his work to inspire people. He states, "If you work hard enough and assert yourself, and use your mind and imagination, you can shape the world to your desires." The "working hard" part is the key: "Practice isn't the thing you do once you're good; it's the thing that makes you good."

Through his books, Gladwell has done what he advises other people to do—use one's ideas and efforts to make positive changes. Time magazine has named him one of the one hundred most influential people in the world.

Marie Curie

You must be an exceedingly clever
scientist to win a Nobel Prize
in chemistry or physics. There is
one person who won a Nobel
Prize in both of these sciences.
What's more, she was a woman
and she lived in an era when
women were definitely not taken
seriously in the world of science.

Marie was born in Poland in 1867 to a family of famous teachers, and seemed set to have an easy life. But her mother and sister both died when she was a little girl, and her family lost all their money supporting Polish independence groups.

As a teenager and young adult, Marie, who was extremely intelligent, had to take whatever kind of work she could get in order to put herself through school. She worked as a governess, teaching the children of a rich family, and fell in love with their son. The family would not let him marry this penniless woman, and Marie was out of a job again.

She finally moved to Paris, where her sister was living, and where some of the best universities could be found. Marie lived in a bare attic, tutoring at night, going to university in the day, and barely making ends meet.

Her luck changed when she met another science student named Pierre Curie. They married and set up a laboratory together; they both loved science so much that they hardly ever left their lab.

Now Marie Curie's brilliance had a chance to shine. She began looking at radioactivity, which had just been discovered, and set up innovative experiments that proved how radiation came from atoms. It was an enormous breakthrough, and she was still just a student.

In the years to come, she and her husband made more discoveries—including the important fact that uranium is not the only radioactive mineral. In fact, Marie Curie discovered a previously unknown mineral that she named "polonium" in honor of her native Poland.

Although women were not taken seriously in the world of science in the late 1800s, no one could ignore the important discoveries that Marie Curie was making. She and her husband shared the Nobel Prize for Physics in 1903, making her the first woman to ever receive this prestigious award. Then, in 1911, she won her second Nobel Prize, this one for Chemistry.

Marie Curie became the most famous woman scientist of all time, but all of those years working with radiation took their toll. She died of anemia brought on by radiation poisoning when she was sixty-six.

Martin Luther King, Jr.

Martin Luther King, Jr., highly intelligent, well educated, and a believer in the philosophy of Mahatma Gandhi, was the voice of the civil rights movement in the United States in the 1950s and 1960s.

"I have a dream," announced Reverend Martin Luther King, Jr. in his most famous speech. His dream was that one day all people would be treated equally, regardless of their race, color, or religion. It was a dream to which he dedicated his life, and it ultimately led to his murder.

Martin Luther King, Jr. was a highly intelligent young man, and skipped several grades in school before getting three university degrees and becoming a preacher at age twenty-five. The year was 1954, and the civil rights movement was just gaining steam in the United States.

As his fellow African-Americans were beaten or even killed for daring to try to vote or to aspire to the same rights as white people, King became deeply involved in the civil rights movement.

In 1955, he led a boycott of the bus system in Montgomery, Alabama—one of many public transportation systems that required black people to sit at the back and give their seats up for white people.

Dr. King helped organize other religious leaders into a powerful, united voice that opposed racial discrimination, and demanded equal rights and justice. He adopted the philosophy of the great civil rights leader Mahatma Gandhi, who taught that the way to oppose violence was with non-violence, and that quiet, peaceful protests would accomplish more than fighting.

This was not easy to do, since protestors were often violently attacked by police, and many civil rights workers were murdered for their efforts to fight racism.

At marches, sit-ins, boycotts, and other non-violent protests, Dr. King would give impassioned speeches. His calls for justice and equality were so powerful that he inspired many Americans, both black and white, to join his cause. His greatest moment came at a huge march in Washington, D.C. in 1963, where his "I have a dream" speech electrified the whole nation.

In 1964, the United States finally passed a civil rights law, and Dr. King won the Nobel Peace Prize for his part in that victory.

Although Dr. King continued to receive death threats, he kept on fighting for social justice. During his last speech, in 1968, he assured the crowd that black Americans would reach "the promised land" of equality . . .but that he might not get there with them. The very next day, Reverend Martin Luther King, Jr. was assassinated.

He is remembered as the greatest hero of the American civil rights movement.

Martti Ahtisaari

On the basis of his reputation as an avid peacemaker who had been sent by the United Nations to many parts of the globe to help resolve conflicts and support international peace efforts, Martti Ahtisaari was awarded the Nobel Peace Prize in 2008.

Catholics and Protestants fighting in Northern Ireland . . . tensions between Kosovo and Serbia in Central Europe . . . battles between nations and tribes in Africa . . . bloodshed in Indonesia —all of these conflicts have one thing in common—in each case, the opposing sides were brought closer to peace by the same man: Martti Ahtisaari.

Who would have thought that Martti was destined to be a global peacemaker when he was born in a small village in Finland just before World War II? But as a young man, Martti showed a special talent for languages and for teaching—he seemed to be able to reach out to people and help them understand things.

When he took a teaching job in Pakistan, giving English lessons and helping train other teachers, Martti Ahtisaari's eyes were opened to the power of nations to help one another. Upon returning to Finland, he started working for the government, first helping diplomats, and then becoming one himself.

That was when Ahtisaari's ability to speak five languages and his capacity to see all sides of an issue really began to shine. Soon, he was traveling the world, helping to support international peace efforts. At first, he represented his home nation of Finland, but the United

Nations soon recognized his talents and sent him to many parts of the world to help resolve conflicts.

Ahtisaari's work was challenging and sometimes dangerous; he often had to persuade armed and angry groups to calm down enough to talk to one another. On one mission in South Africa, he narrowly escaped being attacked by government agents.

At one point, he turned from peacemaker to politician and was elected president of Finland for six years. He used his position to work with other nations and urge more international cooperation.

Since then, Martti Ahtisaari has continued to work tirelessly for peace, and has created a non-profit group dedicated to ending conflict. In recognition of his success in helping to end violence and to get opposing groups talking, he has been given many major awards. In 2008, he was awarded the Nobel Peace Prize for his efforts in resolving international conflicts.

Ahtisaari likes to point out that conflict is part of everyday life, but so are mediation and the desire for peace. It just depends, he says, on which path you choose to follow.

Mattie Stepanek

Mattie Stepanek was a remarkable child who wrote inspirational poetry, raised funds for muscular dystrophy, and was an advocate and fundraiser for children with disabilities and for world peace.

★ 145 ★

Becoming an internationally known peace advocate at a young age is impressive. Having seven books on the bestseller list is even more remarkable. Doing all of that before the age of fourteen is nothing short of amazing!

Mattie Stepanek did all of that and more—and who knows how much more he could have done if he had lived past his teenage years. Mattie was born with a rare form of muscular dystrophy, a disease that also killed his sister and two brothers in early childhood. In Mattie's case, he was a month short of his fourteenth birthday when he died.

In his few years of life, Mattie made a bigger impact than most people do in an extended lifetime. Although he knew his time on Earth was going to be limited, Mattie was determined to keep a positive and hopeful attitude.

He began writing inspirational poetry when he was three years old to help him cope with his brothers' deaths. The poems were so beautiful that his mother sent them to a publisher. That book, and six more collections of poems and essays by Mattie, became bestsellers and brought comfort to millions of readers.

All of Mattie's writing was based on his belief that each of us has a "heart song"—a special gift that we can give to others, and that this gift is the reason we were born.

Mattie used the fame he earned from the success of his poetry to help raise funds for fighting muscular dystrophy, and to become an advocate for world peace and for aid for children with disabilities. He made a wide circle of friends and supporters, including Oprah Winfrey and country singer Billy Gilman.

Although he had such a short life, Mattie's beliefs and work live on after him. The many foundations and programs dedicated to his memory have helped literally millions of people around the world through scholarships and programs for peace. His poetry has been set to music and performed at major concert halls. There are peace gardens, exhibits, and statues commemorating his life and his philosophy that all the world needs is "just peace."

At Mattie's funeral, former U.S. President Jimmy Carter said that he had met kings and queens, presidents and prime ministers, but that the most remarkable person he had ever met in his life was Mattie Stepanek.

Maude Abbott

Maude Abbott wanted to
become a doctor at a time
when women were not allowed
to study medicine. Eventually,
she became not only a doctor
but also a world-renowned
expert on heart disease.

In the late 1800s, women in Canada were supposed to become wives and mothers. A few might be nurses or primary school teachers, but most careers were closed to them simply because of their gender. This kind of sexism was common around the world.

Things were just starting to change when Maude Abbott was born in Quebec in 1869, only two years after Confederation. Although she came from a famous family (her cousin, James Abbott, became prime minister), Maude had a difficult childhood. First her father abandoned the family and then her mother died, and she was raised by her grandparents.

Maude was a very bright girl who dared to dream of achieving something more than a traditional role. She wanted to become a doctor. However, although she was admitted to university (she was part of only the third class of women at McGill University), Maude Abbott was not allowed to study medicine because she was a woman.

Eventually, she found a school that would let her earn her medical degree. Then, she went on to study in Europe. With all of that education and her powerful brain, Maude Abbott became more than just a doctor—she became a medical genius!

Back in Canada, Dr. Abbott published the first of more than 140 books and papers, most of them on heart disease. Eventually, she was recognized as a world expert in her field. At that point, McGill University accepted her, giving her an honorary medical degree and a job as a professor. She set up their medical museum, which became an important research center.

Dr. Abbott had to fight hard to earn recognition, and she wanted other women to be treated more fairly. She helped found the Federation of Medical Women of Canada to support and encourage women in medicine. She spent so much time helping others, and had so much energy to give, that she became known by the nickname "The Beneficent Tornado."

To this day, Dr. Maude Abbott is still helping young women and all medical students—through her books, the McGill museum, and the scholarships awarded in her name. She was a medical pioneer and a giant in the field of heart disease, but it is her generous spirit as much as her accomplishments that keep her memory alive today.

Maya Angelou

Though her life as a child and teenager was dark and difficult, Maya Angelou emerged to become a world-renowned writer as well as a poet, dancer, singer, songwriter, film director, and activist.

Maya Angelou has a straightforward philosophy of life: "If you don't like something, change it. If you can't change it, change your attitude."

You can see the results of that thinking in the remarkable path of her life, which has taken her from a childhood of abuse and broken homes, through teenage years marked by prostitution and crime, to her current life as one of the most respected writers in the world.

Maya Angelou was almost lost for good during the early, dark times of her life. She was sexually abused by her mother's boyfriend at age eight and although she had the courage to speak out, her attacker served only one day in jail. He was later found murdered, and Maya suspected her own family had killed the man. The young girl blamed the power of her voice for ending a life, and refused to speak for nearly five years!

This and other tragedies left Angelou a frightened and bitter young woman. She might have sunk into a desperate life of crime for good if it were not for one person—a teacher who introduced her to great books.

Angelou devoured Shakespeare, Dickens, and other classic authors' works, and discovered a love of language and ideas. It renewed her faith in herself and the world, and set her on the path to making the most of her life. She determined to improve the world around her, and to improve herself along the way.

With her strong will and work ethic, Maya Angelou succeeded everywhere—touring the world as a dancer, starring on Broadway as a singer, editing newspapers and magazines, writing songs and composing scores for movies, being nominated for a Pulitzer Prize for her poetry, and becoming the first black woman in the United States to have a screenplay produced and to direct a major film.

Maya Angelou is also a bestselling author. Her autobiographical books, including I Know Why the Caged Bird Sings, have won critical acclaim around the world.

Along the way, Angelou has lived up to her philosophy of trying to bring about positive change in the world. She played a major role in the civil rights movement in the United States, and has dedicated much of her life to fighting racism through education and political involvement.

Maya Angelou changed her attitude as a teenager, and she has since changed the world.

Michael Jordan

Although he was already an outstanding athlete, in Grade 10 Michael Jordan was told he wouldn't be picked for the varsity basketball team— and would never make it as a college or professional player— because he was too short.

It now seems incredible that anyone ever told the boy who would become the greatest basketball player in history that he was never going to make it as a professional, but that is exactly what happened to the legendary Michael Jordan.

Today, Jordan is described by most experts as the best player to ever pick up a basketball. His list of awards, records, scoring titles, most–valuable-player trophies, Olympic gold medals, NBA championships, and other honors goes on for several pages. When the TV sports channel ESPN conducted a poll of sports journalists, they voted Michael Jordan the number one athlete in any sport of the past one hundred years!

Yet in high school, Jordan couldn't even make the varsity basketball team. He was already an outstanding athlete in basketball, football, and baseball, but when he tried out for the senior basketball team in Grade 10, the coaches told him he was simply too short. He was told that, at 5' 11" (183 cm), he was never going to make it as a college or professional player.

Some people might have taken that judgment to heart and lost their self-confidence, but Michael Jordan took it as a challenge, and decided he would prove the coaches wrong. He took his dedication to the sport to the next level, practicing and working out in every spare moment. In Grade 11, Michael was on the basketball team. In Grade 12, he was named one of the best high school basketball players in the United States.

As a star player in university, Michael Jordan had another turning point in his life when he scored the winning basket at the last second in a U.S. college championship game. That boost to his self-esteem never faded, and Jordan says he has never doubted himself since then.

Going on to win more championships at the college and professional levels, and setting records that may never be broken, Michael Jordan traces much of his success back to the lesson he learned in high school—when someone tells you that you can't accomplish something, it simply means that you have to try harder.

Michael Faraday

The son of a blacksmith, born in England in 1791, Michael Faraday was a self-educated genius with a passion for science and invention.

The great genius Albert Einstein used to keep three photographs on his desk: one of Sir Isaac Newton (who discovered gravity);one of James Maxwell (who proved how electricity, magnetism, and light are all related)' and one of Michael Faraday.

That's pretty good company for the son of a blacksmith who had virtually no education.

Michael didn't have much hope of a decent schooling: boys from the lower classes in England in the 1700s went to work, not school. But bright young Michael caught a lucky break when he was apprenticed to a book dealer, and was allowed to read as much as he wanted.

Even though he was self-educated, it was obvious that Michael was highly intelligent. He started going to lectures by a famous chemist, Humphry Davy, and wrote a 300-page book based on Davy's ideas!

The great scientist was flattered and ended up hiring Faraday as an assistant. In those days, a lower-class person like Michael Faraday was not considered a "gentleman"—on a trip to Europe, he had to act as Davy's valet and live with the servants.

Although the odds were against him, and he was often treated unfairly by his social superiors, Faraday kept working hard and earning his way up the ladder of success. In fact, he worked so hard and so brilliantly that his lower-class roots were eventually forgotten, and he became a giant of English science.

His discoveries about the nature of gases, how electricity and light interact, and other fundamental rules of chemistry and physics literally changed the world. The electric motors used around the world today were made possible by Michael Faraday's work. The Bunsen burners you still find in modern laboratories were just one of his inventions.

But Faraday was also a dedicated public servant, and used his great intelligence to help build a better world. He became an expert in preventing explosions in coal mines, in building lighthouses to keep ships safe, and in fighting the industrial pollution ruining England's environment.

The only time he failed to help his country was when he was asked to help invent chemical weapons: the very religious Faraday refused to use his genius for war.

In old age, Michael Faraday was a national hero. A grateful government gave him a free house and income for the rest of his life.

No wonder Albert Einstein looked up to him!

Michael J. Fox

As a teenager, Canadian Michael J. Fox became a Hollywood star and his acting career took off like a rocket. But at the height of his career, though still young, he was struck down by Parkinson's disease.

When Michael J. Fox wrote his memoir, he called the book Lucky Man. Some people might have been surprised at that title.

After all, Fox was hit at an early age by Parkinson's disease—a brain disorder that usually affects older people. As a result, he suffers from severe tremors and twitches, painful rigidity, and muscle spasms that get worse every year. The disease pretty much destroyed his highly successful acting career.

But the full title of Fox's book says it all: it is Lucky Man: Adventures of an Incurable Optimist. Fox looks at the bright side of everything, including his disease.

It's easy to see how Michael J. Fox could have been an optimist when he was younger. The Edmonton, Alberta native was only eighteen when his acting career took off and swept him to Hollywood.

After only a few small movie parts, Michael got the opportunity of a lifetime—a key role in a major new TV series, Family Ties. As the character Alex Keaton, he became a major star.

That led to another huge break: the starring role in the Back to the Future films. Soon, he was starring in everything from comedies to romances to action movies, not to mention more leading TV roles in series like Spin City. He even provided the

voice for the animated title character in the Stuart
Little films.

In the middle of all of that success . . . with money,
fame, Emmy Awards and Golden Globes pouring in
. . . Michael J. Fox learned that he had Parkinson's.
Within a few years, the disease was too severe for him
to be able to hide the symptoms, and his high-flying
career crashed down to earth.

While many people would have given in to anger
or despair, Fox focused on the positive impact on his
life, describing his condition as a "gift"—an opportunity, not a life sentence.

He quit drinking, got more involved with his family, and became a powerful advocate and fundraiser
for Parkinson's research. He formed a foundation to
support research and fought against politicians who
want to restrict it. Now the whole focus of his life is
finding a cure for Parkinson's.

Fox has told interviewers that his life has much
more meaning and purpose now, and that he treasures
every day. For now, Parkinson's remains incurable, but
so does the endless optimism of Michael J. Fox.

Michaëlle Jean

Michaëlle Jean has had a variety
of interesting roles in her life.
Compassionate and caring,
she has always used them
to support her advocacy for
freedom, equality, and justice.

The year 1968 was a dangerous and frightening time to live in Haiti. Dictator François Duvalier was jailing and torturing anyone who spoke out against his brutal government.

Many victims and their families tried to escape, and a lucky few made it to Canada. That's how a little girl named Michaëlle Jean wound up in the small Quebec town of Thetford Mines.

She grew into a beautiful, well-educated woman who could speak half a dozen languages. Although Jean now enjoyed a peaceful, prosperous life, she never forgot the suffering she had seen—her father tortured, poor people oppressed, women and children brutalized.

So Michaëlle Jean worked at a women's shelter and with new immigrants to Canada, helping others improve their lives. She began a successful career as a radio/TV broadcaster and filmmaker, and used her position there to shine a light on injustice and suffering around the world.

As she worked to build a network of women's shelters across Canada and write about the hardships of immigrant women, Jean used her remarkable brain, but led with her heart. She became known for her sympathy for anyone fighting on the side of freedom and equality.

Then, in 2005, her reputation for caring and compassion led to an amazing opportunity; a chance to make an even bigger difference in the world. It came in the form of an invitation from the Government of Canada, asking if Michaëlle Jean—the former immigrant girl from Haiti—would like to be the next governor general!

As the Queen's official representative in Canada, she met world leaders, hosted important conferences, and traveled the globe as a spokesperson for the nation.

But most importantly, in this position Jean was able to lead and inspire others to follow her example. As governor general, she dedicated herself to breaking down barriers —between French and English, black and white, rich and poor, east and west, north and south.

After her term as governor general came to an end, Michaëlle Jean was chosen by the United Nations to be a special envoy for her homeland of Haiti, giving her a fresh opportunity to help tackle the challenges in that troubled country.

She continues to lead with her heart, lending her voice and energy to care for the underprivileged, and helping to make the world a better, more caring place.

Mohamed ElBaradei

Elected three times as head of the International Atomic Energy Agency, Mohamed ElBaradei advocates for the peaceful use of nuclear energy and the reduction of nuclear weapons.

"If the world does not change course, we risk self-destruction."

Mohamed ElBaradei believes that nuclear weapons may destroy all the people in the world unless we change our ways. He has dedicated his life to helping the world change course, and choose a smarter way to use nuclear energy.

Growing up in Egypt, Mohamed ElBaradei was inspired by his father, who fought for democracy and free speech. Young Mohamed determined to follow in his father's footsteps and help make a difference.

First as a lawyer, then as a teacher and diplomat, the younger ElBaradei looked for ways to promote peace and justice. Then, in the mid-1980s, his life changed . . . and the whole world would change as a result!

In 1984, ElBaradei got a job with the International Atomic Energy Agency (IAEA), which is a group set up by the United Nations to keep an eye on how countries are using nuclear technology. After a few years, he was promoted to head of the Agency, and he began to transform the way it worked.

ElBaradei secured more power for the IAEA, which allowed it to get tougher on countries that broke the rules. He challenged governments when they tried to lie about their nuclear weapons programs, or to hide problems with their atomic power plants.

Mohamed ElBaradei really stirred things up when he stood up to the United States, which wanted to go to war with Iraq. He insisted that the Americans were wrong about Iraq building nuclear weapons and said war was not justified.

From helping keep nuclear fuel out of the hands of terrorists, to encouraging countries to help each other to fight cancer with nuclear medicine, Dr. ElBaradei has taken on one tough issue after another. The countries of the world have re-elected him to three straight terms as head of the IAEA.

Mohamed ElBaradei has also chalked up one award after another from grateful nations and groups that saw how he was reducing the nuclear threat. In 2005, he and his UN Agency were awarded the Nobel Peace Prize (ElBaradei donated his share of the prize money to building orphanages in his home city of Cairo).

Today, as one of the world's leading experts on the peaceful use of atomic power, Mohamed ElBaradei continues to spread his message. Pointing out that we could feed the entire world by using just one per cent of the money spent on nuclear weapons, he challenges people to choose peace.

Mahatma Gandhi

Mohandas "Mahatma" Gandhi was a peaceful warrior who fought for India's independence, and for social justice for India's people. To the rest of the world, he demonstrated the power of non-violent protest as an effective way to fight oppression.

All over the world, people use non-violent protests to fight for justice—they march, sing, sit, and either refuse to cooperate or to resist when authorities try to move them. This form of protest is popular because it is often successful and because it does not involve violence.

One man is given credit for proving the power of non-violent protests—Mahatma Gandhi.

Nearly a hundred years ago, Mohandas Gandhi (who came to be known later in life as Mahatma, or "great soul") was a lawyer from India who cared deeply about social injustice. He first got involved in protests while working in South Africa, where the Indian population was oppressed along with other non-whites.

On his return to India, Gandhi saw that his country was filled with unfairness, too—classes and castes oppressed each other, and the ruling British imposed their rules on everyone.

With his experience and quietly powerful personality, Gandhi soon became leader of the protest movement demanding fair treatment and Indian independence from England. He knew that violent protests would only give authorities an excuse to crack down on everyone involved, and to arrest or harm protestors.

So, Gandhi developed the idea of non-violent protests. Under his leadership, huge crowds would march vast distances or peacefully occupy a public space. His methods attracted a lot of media attention and embarrassed the authorities, who looked bad in the public eye if they arrested people who weren't even resisting. Gandhi himself staged hunger strikes to back up his demands for justice, often coming near to death.

Through years of struggle, Gandhi and his followers won one battle after another—fairer taxes, less discrimination, better relations between religious groups, less poverty, and more rights for women. But they paid a terrible price, with thousands of people killed or injured by police and soldiers, and tens of thousands arrested.

Gandhi's last struggle, for Indian independence, was the hardest one. He and his family, along with their closest supporters, were imprisoned for years. Gandhi's wife died and the Mahatma himself was nearly killed by malaria.

Independence finally came in 1947, thanks largely to Gandhi's leadership and courage.

But the British cut the nation into two parts, India and Pakistan, sparking violence and starvation that killed hundreds of thousands of people. If Gandhi had not stepped in personally, it would have been even worse.

The Mahatma was assassinated in 1948 while leading a prayer meeting. He died as he lived, seeking peace.

Mother Teresa

How did a young girl from Albania, armed only with compassion, become world-renowned and a winner of the Nobel Peace Prize?

Even when Agnes Bojaxhiu was a little girl in Albania, she had a big heart. She longed to make things better for people, and she wanted to live in India, where she knew there was sickness and poverty.

When she grew up, Agnes decided to become a nun and dedicate her life to helping people in need. As a nun, she took a new name, Sister Teresa, and a new job teaching near the poorest area of Calcutta, India.

She had made her dream come true but wanted to do much more. So she asked for permission to start her own group of nuns. Her group would go right into the slums and take care of the very poorest and sickest people.

Sister Teresa started orphanages and schools for children in need, and treated every child as her own. She also opened hospitals for people who couldn't afford medical care. People started to call her "Mother Teresa," and many were inspired to support her or join her efforts.

But Sister Teresa's big heart demanded she do even more. She personally walked the slums of Calcutta, comforting the people there. She would sit down next to people, hold their hands, or take their faces between her hands and look at them with love.

She even did this with lepers (people suffering from the painful and often contagious skin disease called leprosy). Sister Teresa touched the people no one else would touch—the forgotten people, who needed love most. "There are poor people everywhere," she said, "but the deepest poverty is not being loved."

Her remarkable compassion touched people's hearts, and word began to spread. Newspapers started writing about "The Saint of The Gutters" and, before long, Mother Teresa was known all over the world.

She was given the Nobel Peace Prize for her work but always gave credit to other people and to God. Her advice was to do little things to help others, with love. "There are many people who can do big things," she said, "but there are very few people who will do the small things."

By doing the small things with love, Mother Teresa changed the world. She died in 1997, at age eighty-seven, and many consider her to have been a real-life saint.

Nelson Mandela

After twenty-seven years
in prison, Nelson Mandela
was elected president of his
country. His primary goal
was to convince blacks and
whites of the power and
wisdom of forgiveness.

When Nelson Mandela was young, racism was not only perfectly legal in South Africa, it was the law!

Black people were not allowed to vote, go to the same schools, shop in the same stores, or live in the same areas as white people. The system was called apartheid, and people were jailed if they spoke out against it.

Mandela was one of many people who fought against apartheid. At first, as a young lawyer, he tried to combat it through the legal system. But he got so angry with the beatings, murders, and other mistreatment of black people that he started urging them to fight back . . . to meet violence with violence.

As a result of his actions, he was arrested and sentenced to prison for life. Even in prison, because he was black, he got worse treatment than the white prisoners—poor food, hard labor such as breaking rocks in the hot sun, and only one letter or visitor every six months.

Nelson Mandela spent twenty-seven years in those terrible conditions. In the meantime, the world outside South Africa became more aware of, and more opposed to, apartheid. Around the globe, people and governments demanded justice, including freedom for Mandela.

Finally, the South African government gave in—they agreed to end apartheid, have an election where everyone could vote, and let Nelson Mandela go free.

Over the years, Nelson Mandela had become a symbol of the fight against oppression. Most people expected him to come out of prison angrier than ever; they thought he would call on black people to seek revenge.

But Mandela had spent all those years thinking about everything he had seen, and he had changed his mind about fighting and hating. He wanted to find a way to work together with whites, to build a "rainbow nation" where every person would be equal, like the colors in a rainbow.

In the first free election in South Africa, Mandela was elected president. He worked to get black and white people to forgive each other for bad things they had done in the past.

"If you want to make peace with your enemy, you have to work with your enemy," he said. "Then he becomes your partner."

Nelson Mandela was awarded the Nobel Peace Prize in 1993. The man who had lost so much had taught his nation, and the world, the importance and power of forgiveness.

Norman Bethune

Besides being a medical doctor and an inventor in his field, Norman Bethune was a compassionate and courageous humanitarian who worked on the battlefront not only in World War I, but also in the Spanish Civil War and the Chinese Civil War.

If you visit China, you won't find many statues of non-Chinese heroes. One of the few exceptions is the statue of a Canadian, Dr. Norman Bethune.

Norman came from a well-to-do family but always wanted to help those less fortunate than himself. Going to university in the early 1900s in Toronto, he interrupted his studies twice—once to go and teach English to immigrant mine laborers in northern Ontario, and again to volunteer to carry wounded soldiers on the battlefront in World War I.

Norman had a brain equal to his big heart and, after becoming a doctor, he went on to invent or perfect several tools used in surgery. One of them, the Bethune Rib Shears, is still used today.

While he became a very successful surgeon, Dr. Bethune still devoted most of his time and energy to helping others. During the Great Depression of the 1930s, he treated poor people for free, and tried to convince colleagues and governments to provide better care for the needy.

When fascists tried to seize power in the Spanish Civil War, Dr. Bethune volunteered for the democratic side. He saw many soldiers bleed to death on the battlefields before they could be taken to field hospitals, so he invented the world's first portable transfusion unit, saving countless lives.

Just a few years later, Norman Bethune was volunteering again, this time to help the communist side in the Chinese Civil War, then staying on to help during China's war with the Japanese. He did everything from performing emergency battlefield surgery to establishing training programs for doctors and nurses, and organizing medical services.

Norman Bethune was known for helping anyone who needed him, and for putting the lives and health of others before his own. He died of blood poisoning after cutting his finger while performing an emergency surgery in 1939.

The story of this selfless man might have been forgotten, but Chinese leader Mao Zedong wrote a story about Dr. Bethune and it became required reading in every school in China. Even today, decades after his death, Norman Bethune is remembered and honored across the nation he gave his life to help.

In Canada, Dr. Bethune has been inducted into the Canadian Medical Hall of Fame, been honored with a Canadian stamp, had schools named after him, and been the subject of films and TV shows.

Both nations remember him as a medical pioneer and a noble humanitarian.

Norman Borlaug

Norman Borlaug acted on his conviction that increasing the world's food supply is a huge and essential contributor to world peace.

Ninety-eight people have won the Nobel Peace Prize for their contributions to the human race. Only one of them—Norman Borlaug—is also a member of the U.S. National Wrestling Hall of Fame.

Born to farmers in rural America, Norman was a farmer to his boots—a big, strong youth who loved the land. He might have stayed a farmer all his life, except for two factors. First, he was an exceptional amateur wrestler—a talent that gave him the opportunity to travel and put on exhibition matches. He also credits his wrestling with teaching him to never give up.

Second, he was influenced by his grandfather, who encouraged him to get an education. He told Norman, "You're wiser to fill your head now if you want to fill your belly later on."

So Borlaug worked his way through university, studying forestry. His summer jobs took him around the U.S. during the Great Depression of the 1930s. He saw many people literally starving to death, and he realized how easy it was to take food for granted.

When he heard a scientist lecture about breeding plants to fight disease and parasites, Norman Borlaug put the two ideas together—realizing that breeding better crops could help stop people from starving.

That mission became the focus of his life, and Borlaug left farming and wrestling behind. The star athlete became a star pupil, earning a PhD in plant pathology and genetics.

As a scientist, Dr. Borlaug made one discovery after another, developing new strains of wheat that grew healthier, faster, and easier than existing wheat. Working in Mexico, he helped that country go from being short of wheat to having enough to sell to the world.

Dr. Borlaug then took his improved wheat to India and Pakistan, countries that were facing a major famine. Despite a long list of challenges, including a war between the two nations, Dr. Borlaug got his super crop to produce the best yields ever seen. The terrible famine was greatly reduced, and Norman Borlaug was credited with saving millions of lives.

People called his new ideas about plants a "Green Revolution," and his theories spread around the world, helping to prevent starvation, the destruction of forests, and fighting over food supplies. In 1970, Norman Borlaug was awarded the Nobel Prize in recognition of his contributions to world peace through increasing food supply.

Until his death in 2009, he kept sharing his message that the future of civilization depends on everyone having enough food.

Oprah Winfrey

It may well be that no other person in history has risen so far—from such poverty and despair to such wealth and fame—as Oprah Winfrey.

Born to a single, teenage mother in rural Mississippi, Oprah was raised by her grandmother until the age of six. The family was so poor that Oprah sometimes had to wear dresses made from potato sacks. Things didn't improve much when Oprah went to live with her mother. They lived in a poor neighborhood and struggled to afford decent food and clothes.

It wasn't only the grinding poverty and the open prejudice against black people that made her childhood so tough; Oprah was beaten and sexually abused by family members. At age thirteen, she ran away from home. By fourteen, she was pregnant (her baby died shortly after it was born), and she got involved with drugs and emotionally abusive men.

But Oprah Winfrey had a spirit that would not be destroyed, and a mind that yearned to be free. Out of her troubled past came a young woman determined to learn, grow, and succeed in life.

Oprah became a top student in high school, and started winning public-speaking contests. She was so good at speaking that she won a university scholarship, and so beautiful that she won the state beauty pageant.

Her big break came when a local radio station offered this bright, well spoken, and determined young woman a part-time job in the newsroom. After that, it wasn't long before Winfrey's hard work and talent earned her a spot in television news. She got so involved in her stories, sometimes crying along with guests who were having trouble, that the television station decided to move her to a talk show. Oprah Winfrey never looked back.

Winfrey took a struggling TV talk show in Chicago to the number one spot in the city, then to the top-rated spot in the entire United States. Within a few years, Oprah Winfrey had the most viewers of any talk show in history, and was on her way to launching a series of successful TV and radio shows, magazines, websites, charities, and the world's most influential book club.

A millionaire by age thirty, and now a billionaire, Winfrey is often described as one of the most powerful people in the world, and one of the most generous. Never forgetting her roots, Oprah Winfrey helps people around the world and encourages others to appreciate and share their good fortune.

Paulo Coelho

The most widely published Brazilian author of all time, Paulo Coelho has sold close to 100 million copies of his books and has also been a theater director, an actor, a songwriter, and a journalist.

When Paulo Coelho told his parents he wanted to be a writer, they thought he was crazy—literally. The Brazilian teenager's parents had him committed to an insane asylum! Paulo escaped three times before he was finally released and ready to follow a more normal path through life. He then enrolled in law school, as his parents desired.

But his creative instinct was too strong to be locked away, either behind bars or inside his own life. He had to break free. So Paulo dropped out of school, became a hippie, and traveled around Brazil looking for his inspiration. He found it through music and started writing amazing, strange, and wonderful songs. Soon, Paulo Coelho's work was being recorded by some of the biggest singing stars in Brazil.

Unfortunately, the oppressive military government at that time thought his songs were too subversive because they talked about freedom and defying authority. Coelho was arrested and tortured for his beliefs.

However, nothing would stop him from using his creative powers. Years after his release, Coelho went for a walk— a 500-mile walk along a road in northern Spain.

He used the time to reflect on his life, and he came to the realization that he still wanted to be a writer.

So even though he was now middle-aged, Paulo Coelho started on a new career as a novelist. His first two books went nowhere, but his third book, The Alchemist, made world history. It has sold more than sixty million copies (one of the bestselling books ever written), and holds the world record for being translated into more languages—seventy-one—than any other book by a living author.

Since then, Coelho has written more than two dozen books, sharing his unique world view with readers everywhere. He has also been a pioneer of sharing his work for free—his publisher once caught him pirating his own books online. His greatest life lesson, he says, has been to never surrender your dreams or give up on making them come true. "The secret to life," according to Coelho, "is to fall down seven times, but to get back up eight times."

Paulo Coelho is also an outspoken activist for peace and social justice. He is a Messenger of Peace for the UN, an Ambassador to the European Union for Intercultural Dialogue, and a member of many other organizations that advocate for peace.

Randy Pausch

When computer science professor Randy Pausch was given a cancer diagnosis and told he only had "three to six months of good health left," he prepared a now-famous lecture entitled "The Last Lecture: Really Achieving Your Childhood Dreams."

As the saying goes, sometimes people are like tea bags—you don't know how strong they are until they are in hot water.

Randy Pausch is an example of a seemingly ordinary person who rose to great heights when he was in the greatest trouble. He took the most negative situation and turned it into an opportunity to have a positive influence on the world.

Dr. Randy Pausch was a popular computer science professor at Carnegie Mellon University in Pittsburgh, Pennsylvania. He had won awards for his teaching, and students enjoyed his humor and sharp insights.

In 2006, Dr. Pausch got some terrible news—he had cancer of the pancreas and only had a few months to live.

While some people would be paralyzed by fear or give up in self-pity, Dr. Pausch decided to live his last months to the fullest. One thing he decided to do was to sign up for a special lecture series his university offered. The idea was for professors to share their life's wisdom with students, as if it were the last lecture they would ever give.

Randy Pausch gave his lecture to a packed hall in 2007. He called it, "The Last Lecture: Really Achieving Your Childhood Dreams." Many people called it the greatest performance they had ever seen.

Dr. Pausch spoke about seizing your dreams and not giving up. He offered insights into computer science and working in teams. He cracked his audience up again and again with his jokes. He even did push-ups on stage!

His lecture was so inspiring that people wanted video and audio copies of it. Soon, it was an Internet phenomenon with a million hits in the first month, and Dr. Pausch was asked to write a book about his approach to life. That book, The Last Lecture, became a bestseller and has been translated into forty-six languages.

Randy Pausch spent the last few months of his life, in between medical treatments, making his own childhood dreams come true—practicing with the Pittsburgh Steelers and appearing in a Star Trek movie.

He also appeared on TV many times and gave several more lectures before his cancer killed him in 2008. To the end, his message was the same—seize the time you have, never give up on yourself or your dreams, and never underestimate the importance of having fun.

Richard Branson

When he's not starting up
a business or chasing new
adventures, Richard Branson
can be found tackling problems
like global warming, poverty,
and access to education. He has
donated millions of dollars of
his own money and helped raise
many millions more for charities.

Few people in the world have as much fun and adventure as Richard Branson. He has set world records for hot air balloon trips over the Atlantic and Pacific Oceans as well as for crossing the English Channel in an amphibious car. Branson has ridden motorcycles across deserts, sailed through monster storms, paraglided off mountains, and bungee-jumped over waterfalls.

He counts people like legendary South African leader Nelson Mandela and musician Peter Gabriel among his many famous friends.

Wherever he goes on his world travels, Branson seeks out new experiences, interesting people, and fresh challenges. He also finds new business opportunities—at last count, Richard Branson had more than 400 companies in every field from music and entertainment to airlines, mobile phone providers, green fuels, and a space travel agency!

Not every one of his business ventures has worked out, but enough have succeeded to make Richard a multi-billionaire and one of the richest people in the world.

It's an impressive success story for a man who started off as a failure in school. Suffering from dyslexia (a learning disability in which the brain mixes up the order of letters and numbers), Richard Branson was a terrible student and dropped out of school at age sixteen.

However, he was fearless, open-minded, and knew how to get along with just about anyone. So Branson played to his strengths, and began looking for ways to make money that involved his love of travel and music. He found his first opportunity buying left-over albums from music companies in Europe and selling them in his native England for a profit.

That led to his first music store, a mail-order business, and a music-production company that signed up bands the mainstream labels were afraid to touch. Since then, Richard Branson has never stopped pursuing new ideas, testing the limits, and sometimes breaking the rules.

Now sixty years old, Branson is still taking life as one big adventure. In his words, "You don't learn to walk by following rules. You learn by doing, and by falling over, then getting up to try again."

Robert Munsch

A born storyteller, Robert Munsch loves writing stories for young children, and children love reading them. A bestselling author in both Canada and the United States, he has sold over thirty million books.

His official biography says he grew up in Pittsburgh, Pennsylvania, but Robert Munsch likes to say that he never grew up at all—he's still as much of a kid as ever! That could be the secret that makes him one of the most popular children's writers in the world. Somehow, he has never lost the power of imagination we all had as children.

Using his imagination is what kept Robert going through school, which he found difficult. He was a very bad pupil and never really learned the basic skills of math and spelling. But he could reach into his mind and come out with wonderfully inventive, silly ideas that he turned into poems and stories.

Robert first set out to become a priest, and also studied history and anthropology at university. But along the way, something special happened—he got introduced to children, and the children got introduced to his stories.

Working at a daycare centre to put himself through school, Munsch discovered his amazing storytelling skills and the joy of thinking like a kid again. Incredibly, he did this for ten years, making up one wonderful story after another, day after day, without ever thinking of writing them down!

It was only when he and his wife moved to Guelph, Ontario, and a librarian overheard Munsch's stories that he was convinced to send some of them to a publisher. Just one was accepted, but that got him going as a writer.

At first, his books sold slowly and gained just a little popularity every year. Then, in 1986, he published Love You Forever. It became the bestselling children's book in Canada and the U.S., and Robert Munsch was suddenly a household name!

Twenty-five years later, Munsch still publishes about two books a year and they all sell like crazy. But what he really loves to do is drop in on kindergarten and daycare classes that have written to him. He will just show up, unannounced, and spend a few hours telling stories. Often, he will arrange to stay with a student's family and share a whole day with them!

Everywhere he goes and all the people he meets provide Robert Munsch with more story ideas and more joy. He's never stopped being a kid, and kids never stop loving him.

Roberta Bondar

Little did Roberta Bondar's
parents know when they
watched her playing astronaut
as a little girl that she would be
Canada's first woman in space,
or that she would specialize
in studying the effects of space
flights on people's brains.

Can curiosity take you into outer space? Just ask Roberta Bondar.

Growing up in Sault Ste. Marie, Ontario, Roberta loved learning how the world worked. Her favorite gifts were chemistry sets, and her favorite game was playing astronaut and exploring new worlds in her imagination. She wanted to know about everything, from plants to animals, art to science, sports to fantasy. So, Roberta kept studying and learning new things.

She took degrees in zoology and agriculture at university, but then got into medicine and ended up becoming a doctor of neurobiology, studying how our brains work. As she earned her medical degree, Roberta Bondar became interested in yet another new field—space medicine!

When Canada announced it was starting a space program and looking for potential astronauts, guess who had her application in the mail the next day? There were four thousand top-notch applicants, but Dr. Bondar had the right stuff—brains, fitness, and a love of exploration. She was one of just six people chosen to take astronaut training.

In 1992, Dr. Bondar blasted off aboard the U.S. Space Shuttle Discovery, becoming Canada's first woman astronaut. She was also the first neurologist to go into space.

After her mission, Roberta Bondar's curiosity about life in space landed her a new job—heading up an international team studying the effects of space flight on people's brains. And she worked with experts around the world to use her new knowledge to help treat diseases here on Earth.

Meanwhile, Dr. Bondar kept questioning, wondering, and getting excited about new topics. She became an expert photographer (her pictures have been shown at the National Gallery), an educator (Chancellor of Trent University), and a pilot.

Because she has done so many interesting things, Roberta Bondar is also a popular speaker and writer, sharing her love of learning and exploring.

Her accomplishments have won her a long list of awards and honors, including induction into the Canadian Medical Hall of Fame and the Order of Canada, and her picture has been on a Canadian postage stamp. Apparently, curiosity can take you into space . . . and to a lot of other interesting places too.

Roger Bannister

After two years of intense training, Roger Bannister became the first person to beat the four-minute mile and the most famous runner in the world. It was an amazing achievement, but not his destiny; he was already working on his next dream.

Imagine setting a world record and becoming one of the most famous people in sports history. Now imagine thinking "That's not enough!" and setting out to become a neurologist.

That's the life story of Roger Bannister, the English runner who was the first person in the world to run a mile in less than four minutes.

Roger didn't set out to be a world-class runner. He never even tried long-distance running until he was seventeen, but he immediately showed talent and Britain asked him to be on their Olympic team in 1948. But Bannister wanted more time to practice, and waited four years until the 1952 Olympics.

The result? Heartbreak! He finished in fourth place, just out of the medals. He seriously thought about quitting running forever.

Instead, he took a deep breath and decided to go after a different dream—the four-minute mile. It was a goal that top runners around the world had been edging closer and closer to, but Roger Bannister determined to beat them all.

After two years of intense training, he was ready. At a track meet in 1954, Roger ran like no other human being ever had. At the finish line, his time was half a second under four minutes. The crowd went wild and the news flashed around the world!

Roger Bannister had another moment of global glory a few months later, when he raced against and beat the Australian runner who had passed his world record. It was called the Miracle Mile, and it confirmed Bannister as the most famous runner in the world.

But fame was not enough for Roger Bannister. He wanted to make a difference through his work as a doctor. He became a neurologist and a top medical expert on the brain, introducing new procedures and conducting research that was published in medical journals around the world. He still loved sport, and successfully worked for sports funding across Britain and for the first steroid testing of athletes.

How did Roger Bannister accomplish so much? Here's his philosophy, in his own words—"Every morning in Africa, a gazelle wakes up. It knows it must outrun the fastest lion or it will be killed. Every morning in Africa, a lion wakes up. It knows it must run faster than the slowest gazelle, or it will starve. It doesn't matter whether you're a lion or a gazelle— when the sun comes up, you'd better be running!"

Roméo Dallaire

Roméo Dallaire went through a horrific experience that changed his life and almost destroyed it; but since that time, he has been a tireless international advocate for a number of critical global causes.

In 1983, the African nation of Rwanda was in bad shape. The two main tribes, the Hutus and the Tutsis, were arguing over how to share power, and people were afraid there would be a civil war.

In fact, something even worse was about to happen—genocide. Genocide is the attempt by one group of people to completely wipe out another group, as the Nazis tried to do to the Jews in World War II.

The United Nations had troops in Rwanda to try to keep the peace, and Canadian General Roméo Dallaire was put in charge of the troops. He didn't have many soldiers and his orders were to supervise a peace, not fight a war.

But Dallaire and other observers could see the situation was getting worse. Radical Hutu leaders were talking about killing every Tutsi—even the children—and anyone else who got in their way. Dallaire asked for more troops to prevent a bloodbath, but the United Nations argued and debated instead of acting. The general still had a terrible shortage of troops when the killings began.

It was a horrific time, with gangs of armed Hutus massacring whole Tutsi villages. General Dallaire used his troops as best as he could to guard areas where there were Tutsis hiding. He often bluffed the Hutu militias into thinking he had more soldiers or authority than he really did.

The terrible slaughter went on for one hundred days and an estimated one million people were murdered before the United Nations finally sent in enough troops to bring peace. For Roméo Dallaire, it was one hundred days of danger, horror, and frustration. But he would not give up, and he did everything he could to stop the violence. It has been estimated that his brave actions saved some 32,000 lives.

Afterwards, however, he suffered from post-traumatic stress disorder (PTSD)—a deep depression that often affects soldiers and other people who have been through horrific situations with loss—and in this case, massive loss—of human life. At one point, General Dallaire even tried to kill himself.

Today, Roméo Dallaire is a decorated hero, an Officer of the Order of Canada, a member of the Canadian Senate, and an outspoken advocate who has devoted his life to several causes—fighting racism, helping people who suffer from PTSD, and working to stop the use of children as soldiers. He has demonstrated two important forms of bravery, facing up to external dangers and his own internal demons.

Ryan Hreljac

Not many seven-year-olds decide to buy a well in an African village, and not many create a foundation to raise millions of dollars for clean water.

Ryan Hreljac seems like your typical Canadian teenager. He goes to school, plays hockey, and likes video games. But Ryan also happens to be the founder of an international foundation that has helped save tens of thousands of lives!

When he was growing up in Kemptville, Ontario, Ryan heard a story from his Grade One teacher. She explained how millions of people in under-developed countries die every year because they don't have access to clean water.

Lots of kids hear about issues like this; only a very few decide to do something about it. Ryan Hreljac was one of these.

Ryan did extra chores at home to earn pocket money. He worked very hard and, over four months, managed to earn seventy dollars. That was enough to pay for a new well in a village in Uganda.

The charity that built the well was surprised to get a donation from a seven-year-old and began telling people about this big-hearted boy. Ryan soon had other children and adults asking him how they could help him solve the world's clean water challenge.

Other charities got involved, the Government of Canada offered to help, and before he knew it, Ryan's single donation was growing into an organization.

With the support of his family, Ryan dedicated all of his free time to the "Ryan's Well Foundation." Eleven years later, that Foundation is still going strong, and it has raised millions of dollars. It has built more than 600 water and sanitation projects in sixteen countries in Africa, helping bring clean water to nearly 700,000 people!

Ryan has received a long list of awards, medals, and honors, met with world leaders and celebrities, and had his message featured on the Oprah Winfrey Show. But when you ask him about his accomplishments, Ryan says, "I'm just your regular, average kid." Ryan Hreljac has demonstrated how anyone can turn their concern into action, inspire others to get involved, and make a real difference in the world.

And Ryan's original well? It is still pumping clean water in that village in Uganda, serving thousands of people every day.

Sam Walton

Sam Walton had a dream: to
own his own department store.
It was a long and winding
road to reach his goal, but
he was committed, smart,
innovative and, above all, a
hard worker. The result? The
Wal-Mart empire now has 9,000
stores in fifteen countries.

Many people consider Sam Walton to be the smartest businessman in history. He was certainly one of the most successful: starting from one store, he created the Wal-Mart chain, the largest retail business in the world. He also invented the Price Club and Sam's Club chains of discount stores.

Before he died in 1992, Sam was the second-richest man in the world, behind only Bill Gates!

His achievements are even more impressive when you know that Sam was born on a small farm in Oklahoma and raised during the Great Depression of the 1930s, when worldwide economic disaster created widespread unemployment and poverty.

For young Sam, it meant working before and after school to earn extra money for his family, then working his way through university to pay for his tuition. He took every job he could find, from waiting tables to delivering newspapers. In between, he served as a military cadet leader, Sunday school volunteer, class president, and starting quarterback of the football team!

Despite the huge extra demands on his time, Sam was a top student, earning a spot in the U.S. National Honors Society. It's not that he was smarter than everyone else; he just worked harder.

After university, Sam Walton got a job working in a department store and dreamed of one day owning his own shop. After serving in World War II, he used his Army pay to lease a store that was part of a franchise chain. He built it up into such a huge success that the franchise owner bought Walton out and took the store back for himself.

Now that he had more money to work with, Sam Walton finally realized his dream of owning a department store. It was the first step towards the Wal-Mart empire that now boasts nearly 9,000 stores in fifteen countries and employs more than a million people.

Walton developed ideas we take for granted today, but were great innovations at the time—discount pricing, extended hours, numerous cash registers, profit-sharing with employees, and involvement in community activities.

Sam Walton said the secret to his success were plain hard work and ten simple rules:

1. Commit to your goals
2. Share your rewards
3. Energize your colleagues
4. Communicate all you know
5. Value your associates
6. Celebrate your success

7.   Listen to everyone
8.   Deliver more than you promise
9.   Work smarter than others
10. Blaze your own path

Sandford Fleming

Sandford Fleming was a
whirlwind inventor whose
ideas came to benefit not
only his home country but the
world. Canadians can thank
him for his "crazy" vision of
building a railway clear across
the vast wilds of Canada.

How many different dreams can one person follow? For Sandford Fleming, it seems there was no limit.

When he was eighteen years old, having just arrived in Canada from Scotland, Fleming was a budding inventor who wanted other active minds around him. So he established the Royal Canadian Institute—a group dedicated to science, invention, and understanding. It still exists today.

Apparently, working as a surveyor and running his new Institute wasn't enough to fully occupy his mind. On the side, Fleming took the time to design Canada's first postage stamp in 1851.

Meanwhile, his tireless energy and sharp mind got him a job as chief engineer of a railway. That's where Fleming developed his next vision—a railway clear across Canada. It took a dozen years for Fleming and others to convince the new Canadian government. Once the government had finally approved the idea, it gave Fleming the job of doing the surveying for the mammoth railway. Fleming had to find the best route from the Atlantic to the Pacific, over hundreds of kilometers of empty prairie and through mountain passes where no one had ever climbed.

He finished the survey job by 1876, and the railway was finished in 1885. Fleming was on hand when they drove the last spike to join the rail lines—and Canada—together.

You might think that institutes, railways, postage stamps, and submarine telegraph cables (he proposed the idea to connect the British Empire through communications) would be enough for one mind. But Sandford Fleming had yet another world-changing idea.

After missing a train in Ireland, Fleming became fed up with the way people kept time. At that time, time was strictly a local affair; every town had its own clock. Twelve noon in one place might be 12:15 in another just up the road. Fleming came up with the idea of creating standard time zones—twenty-four of them around the world. In each zone, the time would be exactly the same. It seems like common sense today, but Fleming had to fight for years to get this idea accepted, and the twenty-four time-zone idea wasn't agreed upon until years after his death.

But Fleming's many achievements were recognized while he was still alive; he was knighted by Queen Victoria. Today, Sir Stanford Fleming is recognized as the father of standard time and of our national railway—a man who changed our nation and the world.

Shania Twain

Shania Twain's long, slow road to fame included poverty, many disappointments, and a terrible tragedy. But when she finally succeeded, she set records that would be the envy of any singer.

Life was tough for little Eileen Edwards (Shania Twain's original name) and her family in the northern Ontario town of Timmins. Her mother and stepfather did not work much and the family often went hungry. Her mother once drove the children more than 400 miles to get help from a food bank in Toronto.

Eileen grew up working hard—hunting, chopping wood, and helping her stepfather plant trees. But she had a special way of earning some extra money: Eileen could really sing. When she was as young as eight years old, she would go into town late at night and sing for coins people would throw for her. She began to write her own songs and dream of becoming a rock star.

Eileen performed in bands as a teenager, touring all over Ontario and developing her talent. Times were still tough; sometimes she could only pay for singing lessons by cleaning her vocal coach's house.

The young singer was hit by one disappointment after another. Twice she went to the U.S. to try out for record companies, but came home empty-handed. Little jobs singing on other people's albums never led to a big break. But Eileen kept on trying, again and again.

Then, Eileen's parents were killed in a car accident. There was no one to take care of her half-brothers and half-sister. So Eileen moved back in with them, and supported her family by singing at a local resort.

She was dirt poor once more, but still would not give up her dreams. When her half-siblings were grown, Eileen tried yet again. She sent her best songs and music samples to more record companies.

Finally, her years of persistence paid off and she was asked to make her first album. Eileen created a new stage name for herself: using an Ojibwa word for "on my way"' and her stepfather's last name, she renamed herself Shania Twain.

Shania Twain went on to make the best-selling album ever by a female singer and the top-selling album in country music history. The singer who kept on trying has now sold sixty-five million albums around the world.

Shirin Ebadi

Under a regime where dissidents and intellectuals often disappeared or were murdered, Shirin Ebadi, Iran's first woman judge, showed enormous courage in spite of death threats, harassment, and imprisonment.

In 1948, things were a lot different in Iran than they are now. If she had the brains and determination, a girl like Shirin Ebadi, born to an educated, well-to-do family, could look forward to going to university and having a good career. Shirin had plenty of both, and she grew up to be a lawyer and a judge, the first woman in Iran to ever preside over a legislative court.

But in 1979, there was a revolution in Iran and very conservative religious leaders took power. Things were about to get very bad for women, girls, and anyone who spoke up against the government. The new leaders declared that women should not be judges and demoted Shirin Ebadi to a secretarial position. She tried fighting the ruling, but eventually just resigned.

It took years of more fighting before the government would recognize her law degree and let her practice as a lawyer. By that time, Ebadi was angry—she was angry over the way she had been dealt with, and the way that all women and children were being treated in Iran.

Despite the dangers of opposing the government (people who protested were often arrested or simply disappeared), Ebadi set out to fight for justice and equality. She wrote books and articles, fought to change the legal status of women and children, took on cases involving dissidents who were in trouble with the government, and helped get a more liberal president elected in Iran.

But women and children were still second-class citizens, and anyone who spoke out against the government could still find themselves in deep trouble. In 2000, there was a series of murders of intellectuals in Iran; Ebadi and others suspected the killers were government thugs. They were right, but it took a long, hard struggle to prove their case, and Ebadi wound up in jail for daring to ask questions.

The more that Shirin Ebadi stood up for her beliefs, the more death threats and harassment she suffered. Finally, she was forced to flee Iran and now lives in exile in Canada. However, she has not stopped speaking out and campaigning for reforms in Iran and other countries where children and women are not treated as equals to men.

Her courageous fight for justice has won her admirers and enemies around the world, as well as the Nobel Prize for Peace.

Stephen Leacock

Though he was a political scientist and economist, Stephen Leacock is not known for his writing on those subjects; rather, he is famous for his sense of humor and his witty stories that continue to inspire writers and comedians today.

A good sense of humor can get you through just about anything; if he were still with us, Stephen Leacock would be the first to agree.

A hundred years ago, Leacock was probably the best-known humor writer and most famous Canadian in the world. His stories and books, such as Sunshine Sketches of a Little Town, had brought him fame and fortune. And soon-to-be-legendary comedians like Jack Benny and Groucho Marx were inspired by his writing.

But, as funny as he was, Leacock hadn't always had much to laugh about.

His family moved to the little town of Egypt, Ontario from England, where they had been quite wealthy. However, their Canadian farm failed and his father became an alcoholic who beat his wife and children. It was up to Stephen to stand up to his own father and kick him out of the house.

A top student, Stephen had to put himself through university by taking teaching jobs, which he hated. He started trying to sell his stories to magazines as a way of making extra money for school—his real interests were economics and politics.

Leacock eventually became head of the political economy department at McGill University in Montreal. By that time, his stories had taken off and his fame had begun to spread worldwide.

Even then, Leacock had a hard time. He had married a wealthy young woman and they tried for fifteen years to have a child. Then their only son was born with a birth defect, and Leacock's wife died of cancer just ten years later.

Through all of his personal problems, and despite the frustration of having his political science and economic work ignored compared to his funny stories, Stephen Leacock kept his remarkable sense of humor.

That humor not only got him through some dark times, it also assured him a place in history. Every year, the Stephen Leacock Award is given to the funniest writer in Canada, and Leacock's books are still found in classrooms and libraries across the country—not his dry works on politics and economy, but the collections of witty tales and parodies that preserve his reputation as a man who made the world laugh.

Terry Fox

Life as he had known it ended
for Terry Fox when he was
twenty. But in the face of tragedy,
he created a dream that inspired
a nation. And his dream lives on.

When a teenager gets cancer and then loses a leg at age twenty, you might forgive him for giving up on any big dreams. But Canadian Terry Fox refused to give up. In fact, he started dreaming bigger than ever.

Terry was determined to raise money for cancer research to help other young people. So he decided to do something no one had ever done before—to run some five thousand miles across Canada, from the Atlantic to the Pacific, on one real and one artificial leg.

Terry prepared for eighteen months, running over 3,000 miles (5,000 kilometers).

He set out quietly on April 12, 1980, dipping his artificial leg in the ocean waters off Newfoundland. Starting that day, and every day that followed, he ran twenty-five miles. Through rain and shine, despite pain and exhaustion, from early morning darkness to long after sunset, he ran the equivalent of a marathon every day.

By halfway through his run, Terry had captured the hearts of his nation. Huge crowds appeared by the sides of remote highways to cheer him on. He visited the notorious Kingston Penitentiary and the hardened inmates wept at his courage and determination.

Sadly, Terry was not able to finish his heroic run. His cancer spread to his lungs, and he was forced to quit on September 1, 1980, near Thunder Bay,

Ontario, after running for 143 days and 3,339 miles (5,373 kilometers).

Terry's goal was to raise one dollar for every Canadian to fund cancer research, a total of $24 million. When Terry had to quit his run, his courage inspired a groundswell of support from across Canada, and the fundraising efforts continued. By February 1, 1981, Terry's Marathon of Hope had raised the $24 million.

Terry lived to see his dream realized, but on June 28, 1981, at the age of twenty-two, Terry Fox died of the disease that he had battled so hard against.

Terry inspired new dreams and new commitment as Canadians followed his example and continued to raise money for cancer research through Terry Fox Runs. In 1988, the Terry Fox Foundation was established to coordinate and manage Terry's legacy. As of Spring 2011, close to $500 million had been raised for cancer research, and over 5,000 locations in Canada were planning a Terry Fox Run for September.

Terry Fox is remembered by Canadians as their greatest hero of all time, and the best example of courage in action.

Thomas Edison

Being an inventor, says Thomas Edison, is not all about having great ideas; it's mostly about working hard and never, never giving up.

Thomas Edison is known as one of the greatest inventors in history—the light bulb, the phonograph, the world's first movie, the stock ticker, the talking doll—more than a thousand different patents have his name on them! There's no doubt that Edison had a very sharp mind. But the man who was called a genius by the whole world said his success didn't have much to do with being smart; he put it all down to hard work.

And it is true that few people in the world work as hard as Thomas Edison did. He was known for working half the night and falling asleep at his workbench. If he had a problem to solve, he would skip meals and go on a few hours of sleep for weeks on end.

Edison simply never gave up. He would keep working, no matter how long it took, until he found the best way of doing things.

His gift for inventing and his determination to succeed almost went unrecognized. Growing up in the 1800s, Edison had seemed doomed to fail. He had two problems that caused him real trouble in school.

First, he was very hard of hearing (this was before hearing aids were invented). Second, he just couldn't seem to focus and sit still. These days, teachers would identify him as having a learning disability; back then, they just said he was unteachable.

So, his mother pulled him out of school at age ten and set out to teach him herself. She knew that her son was much smarter than his teachers thought. And she saw that he never stopped thinking about better ways to solve a problem.

In his first job, when he was a teenager, Edison was taught how to use a telegraph. He saw that it could be improved, so he was soon inventing new and better telegraph machines. The perfect example of his approach is his most famous invention, the light bulb. Edison tried more than a thousand different ways of getting electricity to make light. He refused to stop trying until he found the material that worked.

As Edison liked to say, "Genius is one percent inspiration and ninety-nine percent perspiration." In other words, having a good idea is just the beginning: it's the effort you put behind that idea that gets the results.

Walt Disney

Sometimes it just takes one
good idea to get started on
the road to fame, but the good
idea often comes after many
years of hard work and many
bumps along the road.

Through his whole remarkable life, Walt Disney would always tell people, "It all started with that Mouse." He was talking about Mickey Mouse— Walt Disney's most famous creation and the one that led to what has been called the most successful entertainment company in the world.

Walt Disney loved drawing as a boy, and was determined to be a cartoonist when he grew up. But getting a job drawing cartoons for a newspaper or ad agency turned out to be harder than he thought, and Disney struggled for many years.

While he was working at one agency, he became interested in the new methods of animation. He started to experiment with cameras and drawings, and he was convinced he could make a living as an animator.

After more years of hard work, Walt Disney finally hit it big. He and his crew came up with a character called "Oswald the Lucky Rabbit." Oswald cartoons were a hit, and Disney's studio was finally making money. Then, the company that distributed his cartoons pulled a fast one; it seemed they had the legal rights to Oswald and they forced Walt Disney out.

So he had to start all over again. This time, Walt Disney came up with an even better idea—a mouse he called "Mortimer." His wife didn't like that name, and suggested "Mickey" instead, and so the most popular cartoon character in history was born.

With his first sound cartoon, "Steamboat Willie starring Mickey Mouse," Walt Disney began to make a lot of money. He used it to hire the best animators and writers he could find, and a string of classic characters followed—Donald Duck, Goofy, Pluto, the Three Little Pigs singing "Who's Afraid of the Big Bad Wolf," and many more.

Disney and his team went on to revolutionize movies with the first full-length animated feature, Snow White and the Seven Dwarfs, followed by a string of hit films that continues to this day. Walt Disney was nominated for fifty-nine Oscars, and won twenty-six of them (both record numbers); he also won seven Emmy Awards for his television shows and specials.

One successful idea followed another, including theme parks Disneyland and Walt Disney World— although Walt Disney died just before the second park was opened.

After his beginnings as a struggling young artist, Walt Disney ended his life with great wealth, a world-wide reputation, and the satisfaction of bringing joy to millions of children—all because of a mouse and the tenacity to hang on his dreams.

Wangari Maathai

Some people, by their nature, ignore the status quo and ignore the odds, and go where no one has gone before. They are peaceful but courageous warriors.

Wangari Maathai was the first woman to do a lot of things: she was the first woman from East Africa to earn a PhD, the first woman to head up a department at the University of Nairobi, and the first African woman to win the Nobel Peace Prize.

As a girl in a poor country, Wangari had to work against the odds to achieve these things, but she was never the kind of person to let high odds hold her back. By the mid-1970s, Wangari Maathai was a professor of anatomy, head of the Kenyan Red Cross, and involved in a number of charities and causes. But she was about to get a great idea....

Dr. Maathai could see that Kenya had two major problems—its natural environment was in bad shape, mostly due to too many trees being cut down, and there were so few jobs that many families were struggling or even starving.

Her idea was simple but brilliant: solve both problems at once by hiring unemployed people to plant more trees! This straightforward plan grew into a whole campaign to teach the people of Kenya to understand and respect the environment and each other. She called it the Green Belt Movement.

Although she went through a lot of hard times and struggled with opposition from the Kenyan government, Wangari Maathai managed to keep the Green Belt Movement alive. Then, in 1985, the United Nations held an environmental conference in Kenya, and representatives from many nations were able to see and hear what she was doing. That's when the Green Belt Movement really took off, spreading across Kenya and Africa, and serving as a role model for many nations.

Over the years, Dr. Maathai's group began to stand for other issues as well as the environment—issues like democracy and justice. Kenya only allowed one political party to exist, and tried to deny or stifle anyone who protested or pointed out problems.

Throughout the 1990s, Wangari Maathai and her supporters fought for broader democracy. She was threatened, arrested, beaten, and jailed—but never silenced. It took more than a decade of struggle, but finally Kenya had democratic elections with many parties represented.

Dr. Maathai was eventually elected to the national parliament, won the Nobel Peace Prize in 2004, and planted a tree with Barack Obama. Today, she continues to work for the causes she is known for—people and the environment.

Wayne Gretzky

They told him he was too
small, too slow, and too weak.
But what those coaches and
scouts from thirty years ago
did not realize was that Wayne
Gretzky was unstoppable.

From the time he learned to skate at age two, in his father's backyard rink in Brantford, Ontario, Wayne loved hockey. He would skate, practice, and play hockey every spare moment, even gobbling down his dinner while wearing his skates so that he could rush back out to the ice again and play until dark.

Gretzky credits his father with teaching him the secrets to success, in hockey and in life—to work hard and make the best use of your strengths.

Wayne Gretzky was neither the biggest nor fastest hockey player on any of his teams. In fact, he was usually much smaller than the other players because he would play against older boys. And this seemed only fair—at age six, Wayne could outplay any ten-year-old!

Despite his lack of size and speed, Wayne had such phenomenal talent in passing the puck, making plays, and avoiding the checks of the larger players that he became a child hockey star. He set records and won scoring championships everywhere he went.

But the so-called experts dismissed Wayne's skills and said he could not make it in the stronger, tougher competition of the National Hockey League (NHL). Several teams passed over the chance to sign him up; it was a decision that every one of them would come to regret.

Over a twenty-year NHL career, Wayne Gretzky broke every record in the book. By the time he retired in 1999, he held forty regular-season records, fifteen playoff records, and six All-Star records. With more than thirty NHL awards and trophies, including four Stanley Cup championships, Gretzky's entry in the official record books is longer than that of any other hockey player.

Some of his records may never be broken; no other player has ever scored 200 points in a season, something that Wayne did four times! He capped his incredible career in 2002 by coaching Canada's Olympic hockey team to its first gold medal in fifty years.

When Wayne Gretzky stopped playing, every single team in the NHL retired his number—there will never be another number 99 in the NHL. Today, the hockey experts no longer talk about his lack of size or speed. They simply call him "The Great One."

William "Billy" Bishop

Air Marshal Billy Bishop was a daring World War I fighter pilot who won the Military Cross, the Distinguished Service Order, and the Victoria Cross, and he became the leading Canadian flying ace with seventy-two air victories.

When Billy Bishop was fifteen years old, he did something really stupid. He built an "airplane" out of
cardboard, wood, and string, and then tried to fly it
off the roof of his three-storey house.

His sister dug him out of the wreckage, and was
surprised to find he was not hurt! But Billy was a very
tough boy. He was known as a fighter at school, and he
used his fists to protect other kids from bullies.

When World War I started, Billy Bishop dropped
out of school to enlist in the army. His trainers were
astounded to see what a great shot he was with a rifle;
he seemed like a natural soldier!

But on the battlefields of Europe, Bishop was
soon fed up with living in a muddy, filthy trench. WWI
was the first war in which airplanes were used, and
when Bishop saw an airplane land, he quickly transferred to the air force, hoping for more action.

And action was what he got. Billy Bishop turned
out to be as natural at flying as he was at fighting and
shooting. After flying scouting missions, he asked to
be stationed in France, where British and German
fighter pilots were battling for control of the skies.

At that point in the war, the Germans were shooting down the British by a ratio of five to one. The
average British pilot lasted only eleven days! But the

Germans had never seen anyone like Billy Bishop in action.

Bishop would always lead the way and be the first to attack, no matter what the odds. He frequently returned with his plane shot full of holes. Apart from his regular missions, he would take off alone and fly deep into enemy territory to stage surprise attacks.

Soon, Bishop had shot down five enemy aircraft, then ten, twenty, thirty! His victories kept mounting until the Germans nicknamed him "Hell's Handmaiden" and put a reward out for anyone who could shoot him down.

No one ever did, and Bishop finished the war with a chest covered in medals and seventy-two air victories, making him the top Canadian flying ace of World War I. He had used his crazy courage and natural toughness to fight for his country and become a national hero.

Billy Bishop ultimately became an air marshal, the highest rank possible, and head of the Canadian Flying Corps.

William Harvey

Although brilliant William Harvey became the doctor of choice for the wealthy, the nobility, and even the King of England, he never stopped giving free treatments to the poor.

It may seem hard to believe, but until William Harvey came along, even the best doctors in Europe didn't know that your heart pumps blood around your body. The common wisdom was that blood was created by your liver, and the heart pumped air and heat through your body, along with just some of your blood!

So, you can imagine the uproar in 1628 when William Harvey published a book that explained exactly how the entire circulatory system worked, from your heart to arteries and veins. He was completely right, but his work contradicted the belief that had been around for hundreds of years. Many other doctors refused to believe Dr. Harvey, and said his theories were crazy.

William Harvey was a brilliant physician who had astonished his professors at medical school. Almost straight out of university, he was hired as chief physician at St. Bartholomew's Hospital in London, where he provided medical treatment to the poor for free.

Harvey's reputation grew rapidly, and he was chosen to deliver an ongoing series of public lectures to explain anatomy and medicine to the general public. Soon, wealthy people, including members of the nobility, were asking him to be their doctor. He even wound up becoming the personal physician to the King of England!

But when he published his now-famous book on the heart and blood circulation, it looked as if William Harvey might lose everything.

However, Dr. Harvey's critics hadn't counted on his brilliance and tenacity. He proved his theories time and again with experiments that showed how the circulation system worked, and with calculations that proved the impossibility of the theory about blood originating in the liver.

In the end, no one could argue with the powerful evidence; William Harvey had clearly made a huge advance in medical science. Not only did people finally understand how the heart really worked, they also were inspired to copy his style of provable, repeatable experiments.

While Dr. Harvey went on to great fame and fortune as the physician of kings and other rich clients, and as the man who opened the eyes of the world to the wonders of the heart, he never stopped working for the poor. Until he was an old man, he served at St. Bartholomew's Hospital every week, giving free health care to people who could not afford to pay a doctor.

Winston Churchill

"Never give in — never, never, never, never, in nothing great or small." That was the life philosophy of Sir Winston Churchill—the man who many people believe did more than anyone else did to save the world from the Nazis.

Churchill was a brilliant man (the only British prime minister to win the Nobel Prize for Literature), who came from a wealthy and famous family in England. But his childhood was not easy: Winston had a speech impediment and a rebellious nature. He did badly in school and felt unloved by his parents.

Winston Churchill came into his own at military school as a teenager. Although it took him three tries to pass the entrance exam, he became a top student, and the school's fencing champion.

Once in the military, Churchill took every dangerous assignment available and quickly rose up through the ranks. To make extra money on the side, he wrote stories and books about his military campaigns and became a popular author.

After leaving the British Army, Churchill kept working as a war reporter and historian. He gained even more fame when he was captured in South Africa during the Boer War, escaped from prison, and traveled 300 km on foot to rejoin the fighting as a volunteer!

Back home in England, Churchill turned to politics, using his high profile and great speaking ability to become a member of parliament. Despite several political setbacks, he eventually served as a cabinet minister, introducing reforms such as Britain's first minimum wage law and legislation that led to pensions for company employees.

When World War I began, Churchill was in charge of the British Navy . . . but by the end of the war, unable to resist the call of battle, he was again leading troops on the front lines.

When the Nazis, led by Adolf Hitler, began to rise to power in Germany in the 1930s, Churchill was one of the few political voices warning against them. So, when the Nazis started their campaign to conquer the world and British policies were failing, Britain turned to Churchill to lead them.

As prime minister during World War II, Churchill rallied his tiny country to stand up against the strongest military machine ever known. His brilliant tactics, his ability to bring other allies together, and his stirring speeches and radio addresses, were the keys to defeating the Nazis.

Churchill's absolute refusal to give up, even against overwhelming odds, helped to save his and other nations, and made him one of the greatest heroes in British and world history.

Wisdom to Live Your MAGIC!™ provides you with life lessons from 50 of the most amazing teachers in human history. For each teacher the book includes an original portrait illustration, a brief biography, and selected wisdom from that teacher in his or her own words. Each profile also explains the profound life lesson(s) the author gained from that particular teacher. Mentor Vivo Saggezza will show you how to integrate the wisdom of these amazing teachers into your own life.

"Some of the teachers in this book are the expected, like Einstein, Shakespeare and Confucius but I gained some new insights. Others are a surprise, like Dolly Parton, Black Elk and Keats, and after learning more about them, they all belong in this book."
—Wesley Gunderson, Businessman

This collection of teachers is unique. Each teacher provides insights into the human condition and a viewpoint on living in these times, some from the perspective of long ago and others from the perspective of now. They gently advise, in their own words, how to be fulfilled, happy and successful. Some teach by example, some from the result of research and others from their hearts in the most poetic language. Wisdom to Live Your MAGIC! is definitely worth reading. Each article is about 600 words and can be read in a few minutes. This is a book you can taste and savor. Great for the bedside table.

The Teachers:

Dr. Albert Einstein	George Bernard Shaw
Dr. Albert Ellis	George Lucas
Aristotle	George Washington
Benjamin Franklin	Johann W. von Goethe
Bill Gates	Henry David Thoreau
Black Elk	Sir Isaac Newton
Confucius	James Allen
Dale Carnegie	Jeff Bezos
Dr. Dean Ornish	John Keats
Dolly Parton	Joseph Campbell
Eleanor Roosevelt	Kahlil Gibran
Earl Nightingale	Lao Tzu
Ernest Hemingway	Leo Tolstoy
	Leonardo da Vinci

Mahatma Gandhi

Marcus Aurelius

Mark Twain

Dr. Martin Luther King, Jr.

Michelangelo

Mother Teresa

Dr. Muhammad Yunus

Napoleon Hill

Oprah Winfrey

Oscar Wilde

Pearl S. Buck

Ralph Waldo Emerson

Richard Bach

Rudyard Kipling

Socrates

Steve Jobs

Sun Tzu

Theodore Roosevelt

Thomas Edison

Dr. Viktor Frankl

Warren Buffett

William Shakespeare

Sir Winston Churchill

Release Date: March 2012

This book will prove to you that you are gifted, you are powerful and you are important. It provides a map for your journey to live the life you were born to live. Learn how to discover your gifts, how to make the five critical choices and how to use six powerful tools on your journey to Live Your MAGIC! – Release Date: May 2012

Visit our website for Larry's blog and the latest updates: www.liveyourmagic.com

Follow Larry on Twitter: @liveyourmagic

CPSIA information can be obtained at www.ICGtesting.com
Printed in the USA
LVOW121923240212

270297LV00024B/100/P